T~~HE~~ DRAGON

Evgeny Shvarts

translated by

Laurence Senelick

BROADWAY PLAY PUBLISHING INC
224 E 62nd St, NY, NY 10065
www.broadwayplaypub.com
info@broadwayplaypub.com

THE DRAGON
© Copyright 2012 by Laurence Seneick

First printing May 2012
I S B N: 978-0-88145-530-4

Book design: Marie Donovan
Page make-up: Adobe Indesign
Typeface: Palatino
Printed and bound in the U S A

ABOUT THE AUTHOR
AND THE TRANSATOR

Evgeny Lvovich Shvarts (in English, Eugene Schwartz, 1896-1958), like so many writers of fantasy in the Soviet Union, found that the safest haven for his talent was children's theatre and fiction. When the experimental literary group OBERIU was disbanded and its leading members arrested, Shvarts moved his writing to children's magazines and the Leningrad Theatre of the Young Spectator. He became known for an ingenious mixture of folkloric elements with modern themes. For instance, his first play, UNDERWOOD (1928) was about a witch who steals a typewriter. He became the house dramatist for the Leningrad Comedy Theatre, led by the brilliant director-designer Nikolay Akimov, and provided plays for adults that used fairy tales to make political points. When the Nazis besieged Leningrad, Shvarts was evacuated to Central Asia where he wrote his masterpiece THE DRAGON. When the Comedy Theatre returned to Leningrad in 1944, Akimov and Shvarts tried to persuade the authorities that the Dragon was Hitler and his success the Mayor the Allies: they insisted that it would be useful in reconstructing postwar society. However, the censors realized that the play's message is sufficiently ambiguous to refer to any totalitarian leader, including Stalin. THE DRAGON was banned after one performance. Shvarts uses the eternal conflict of Good and Evil to unmask the disguises power dons to perpetuate itself. The play's ending is far from the rosy optimism prescribed by Socialist Realism. One critic even viewed the townspeople as reincarnations of Gogol's dead souls. Certainly, the play suggests that human beings get the leaders they deserve and was not produced until 1962, nearly a decade after Stalin's death. Out of favor, Shvarts aimed his later fairy-tale parables at children and composed screenplays, including an excellent adaptation of *Don Quixote* (1957). THE DRAGON, however, was frequently revived both in the U S S R and abroad and filmed. Many of its lines became proverbial, such as "Do you think it's easy to love people?"

Laurence Senelick is Fletcher Professor of Drama and Oratory at Tufts University and recipient of the Saint George medal of the Ministry of Culture of the Russian Federation for services to Russian art and theater. He has translated *The Complete Plays of Anton Chekhov* (W. W Norton), edited *The American Stage: Writing on Theater from Washington Irving to Tony Kushner* (Library of America) and compiled the Historical Dictionary of Russian Theater (Scarecrow Press). For Broadway Play Publishing Inc he has translated Gogol's INSPECTOR GENERAL and DEAD SOULS, Schiller's LOVE AND INTRIGUE, ANYTHING TO DECLARE? By Hennequin and Veber, and MUSTN'T DO IT! By Jo van IJssel de Schepper-Becker.

CHARACTERS

THE DRAGON
LANCELOT, *a knight errant*
CHARLEMAGNE, *Keeper of the Public Records*
ELSA, *his daughter*
THE MAYOR
HENRY, *his son, private secretary to* THE DRAGON
THE CAT
FIRST AND SECOND WEAVERS
HATTER
MUSICAL-INSTRUMENT MAKER
BLACKSMITH
GIRL-FRIENDS *of* ELSA'S, *three*
SENTRY
GARDENER
FIRST MAN
SECOND MAN
FIRST WOMAN
SECOND WOMAN
LITTLE BOY
DONKEY
PEDDLER
JAILER
FLUNKEYS, GUARDS, TOWNSPEOPLE

ACT ONE

(A spacious, cosy, spic and span kitchen, with a big fireplace upstage. A gleaming flagstone floor. In an easy-chair before the hearth the CAT *is taking a catnap.)*

LANCELOT: *(Enters, looks around, calls)* Landlord! Landlady! Answer me, if you're among the living! Not a soul!...The house empty, the gates ajar, the doors unlocked, the windows wide open. It's lucky I'm a honest man or I'd ransack the place in two shakes, pilfer all the valuables and make a quick getaway—but all I want is a rest. *(Sits)* I'll wait. Master Cat! Do you expect your owners home soon? Hm? Cat got your tongue?

CAT: I've nothing to say.

LANCELOT: And why is that, if it's not a rude question?

CAT: When you're warm and snug, it's wiser to keep your eyes and mouth shut, my dear.

LANCELOT: True enough, but where are your owners?

CAT: Out, which suits me fine.

LANCELOT: Don't you like them?

CAT: I love them with every hair in my fur, every paw, every whisker, but they're about to be victims of a terrible disaster. The only time I get any peace of mind is when they go away.

LANCELOT: Aha. They're about to be victims of a terrible disaster, are they? What kind of disaster? Nothing to say?

CAT: Not a word.

LANCELOT: Why not?

CAT: When you're warm and snug, it's wiser to keep your eyes and mouth shut than to pry into the troubles tomorrow brings. Meow!

LANCELOT: Cat, you alarm me. The kitchen is so cosy, the fire in the hearth has been so carefully laid. I simply refuse to believe that this nice, roomy house is in for trouble. Cat! What's been going on here? Answer me! Come on!

CAT: Leave me be, stranger.

LANCELOT: Listen, cat, you don't know who I am. I'm so buoyant a fellow that, like a cork, I can float through life and never sink. So it's easy for me to bob up in other people's affairs. That's why I've been wounded so often, nineteen flesh wounds, five serious and three mortal. But I'm still alive, because, not only am I as buoyant as a cork, I'm as stubborn as a mule. So tell me, cat, what's been going on here? What if I could save your owners? I've been known to do things like that. How about it? Oh come on now! What's your name?

CAT: Maggie.

LANCELOT: I thought you were a tomcat.

CAT: I am a tomcat, but people are so unobservant sometimes . My owners still can't figure out why I've never had kittens. They say: what's wrong with you, Maggie? Poor dears! I won't say another word.

LANCELOT: At least you can tell me who your owners are!

CAT: Master Charlemagne the County Clerk and his only daughter, the one with such soft paws, the enchanting, beguiling, tender-hearted Elsa.

LANCELOT: And which of them is the victim of the terrible disaster?

CAT: Oh dear, she is, which means we all are.

LANCELOT: And just what is this disaster? Out with it!

CAT: Meow! Listen, for four hundred years now our town's been harboring a dragon.

LANCELOT: A dragon! Great!

CAT: He exacted a tribute from our town. Every year the dragon picks himself a girl. And without so much as a mew, we hand her over to the dragon. And he carries her off to his cave. And we never see her again. Word is that she dies of intense nausea. Fftt! Scat! scat! F-f-f!

LANCELOT: Who's that meant for?

CAT: The Dragon! He picked our Elsa! Damned reptile! F-f-f-f!

LANCELOT: How many heads has he got?

CAT: Three.

LANCELOT: That's normal. And paws?

CAT: Four.

LANCELOT: Well, that's to be expected. With claws?

CAT: Natch. Five claws to each paw. Each claw as long as a stag's antlers.

LANCELOT: No kidding? And are the claws sharp?

CAT: As knives.

LANCELOT: I see. I suppose he breathes flame?

CAT: Yes.

LANCELOT: The genuine article?

CAT: It starts forest fires.

LANCELOT: Aha! Is he scaly?

CAT: Scaly's the word.

LANCELOT: And these scales are probably pretty thick?

CAT: All the way down.

LANCELOT: Right, but how thick?

CAT: A diamond couldn't make a dent.

LANCELOT: I see. I get the picture. Size?

CAT: Big as a church.

LANCELOT: Uh-huh, it all fits. Thanks, cat.

CAT: You planning to fight him?

LANCELOT: We shall see.

CAT: Well, for heaven's sake, do challenge him to combat. He'll kill you, of course, but it'll take forever, and meanwhile we can stretch out in front of the fire and dream of what it would be like if, by some accident or some miracle, one way or another, by fair means or foul, just maybe, by any manner of means, you wound up killing him.

LANCELOT: Thanks, cat.

CAT: Get up.

LANCELOT: What is it?

CAT: They're coming.

LANCELOT: I only hope I take a liking to her. Oh, if only I can take a liking to her! It's such a big help... (*Leans out the window*) I do like her! Cat, she's quite an attractive girl. But look! Cat! Is that a smile? She's cool as a cucumber! And her father is beaming. Have you been pulling my leg?

CAT: No. The saddest thing about this whole mess is that they keep on smiling. Ssh! Good evening! It's time I had my supper, master and mistress dear.

(*Enter* ELSA *and* CHARLEMAGNE.)

LANCELOT: Greetings, good master and beauteous damsel.

CHARLEMAGNE: Greetings, young man.

LANCELOT: Your house looked so inviting, and the gate was unbolted, and a fire was blazing in the kitchen-grate, so I walked in unbidden. Please forgive me.

CHARLEMAGNE: No need to apologize. Our doors are open to all.

ELSA: Please do sit down. Give me your hat, I'll hang it behind the door. I'll set the table right away... Is anything wrong?

LANCELOT: Not at all.

ELSA: You looked as if you were...afraid of me.

LANCELOT: No, no...it's just the way I am.

CHARLEMAGNE: Do sit down, friend. I'm very fond of travellers. That's probably because I've never set foot outside this town my whole life long. Where do you hail from?

LANCELOT: Down south.

CHARLEMAGNE: And did you have lots of adventures along the way?

LANCELOT: Oh yes. I could have lived without some of them.

ELSA. You must be tired. Please sit down. Why do you keep standing?

LANCELOT: Thank you.

CHARLEMAGNE: You can have a nice long rest in these parts. Ours is a very quiet town. Nothing ever happens here.

LANCELOT: Never?

CHARLEMAGNE: Never. Well, last week, it's true, we did have rather a high wind. Almost lifted the roof off one house. But that's not what you'd call an important event.

ELSA: Supper's on the table. Please. What's wrong?

LANCELOT: Forgive me, but... You say that yours is a very quiet town?

ELSA: Certainly.

LANCELOT: But...what about...the Dragon?

CHARLEMAGNE: Oh that...well, we're used to him, after all. He's lived here for four hundred years now.

LANCELOT: But...I was told that your daughter...

ELSA: Sir Traveller...

LANCELOT: My name is Lancelot.

ELSA: Sir Lancelot, forgive me and...don't take this personally, but please, don't bring up the subject.

LANCELOT: Why not?

ELSA: Because it's a hopeless case.

LANCELOT: Is that so?

CHARLEMAGNE: Yes. It is a hopeless case. We just took a walk through the woods and talked it all over, happily and thoroughly. Tomorrow, as soon as the Dragon carries her off, I shall die too.

ELSA: Papa, you don't have to talk about it.

CHARLEMAGNE: That's all I have to say.

LANCELOT: Excuse me, just one more question. Hasn't anyone ever tried to fight him?

CHARLEMAGNE: Not for the last two hundred years. Before that people often engaged him in combat, but he slew all his opponents. He's a brilliant strategist and a superb tactician. He takes his enemy by surprise, bombarding him with boulders from on high, then he lunges straight down on to the head of his assailant's steed and smites him with fire, which completely demoralizes the poor creature. And then he tears the rider to shreds with his claws. So, eventually people stopped standing up to him...

LANCELOT: But didn't the whole town stand up to him?

CHARLEMAGNE: Once.

LANCELOT: What happened?

CHARLEMAGNE: He burned down the suburbs and drove half the residents distracted with poisonous fumes. He's a military genius.

ELSA: Please help yourself to the butter.

LANCELOT: Yes, yes, I will. I have to keep up my strength. And so—please excuse me asking all these questions—nobody tries to stand up to the dragon any more? He's become a complete totalitarian?

CHARLEMAGNE: Certainly not! He's quite decent!

LANCELOT: Decent?

CHARLEMAGNE: Absolutely. When our town was threatened by cholera, the municipal physician asked him to breathe fire on the lake and set it a- boiling. The whole town drank boiled water and was saved from the epidemic.

LANCELOT: Was this a long time ago?

CHARLEMAGNE: Oh no. At most eighty-two years ago or so. But good deeds are hard to forget.

LANCELOT: And what other decent things has he done?

CHARLEMAGNE: He rid us of the gypsies.

LANCELOT: But gypsies are very nice people.

CHARLEMAGNE: How can you say that! That's terrible!
I admit I've never seen a gypsy in my life. But I was
taught in school that they're awful people.

LANCELOT: Why?

CHARLEMAGNE: They're vagrants by nature, it's
in their blood. They're enemies of law and order,
otherwise they'd settle down and not roam all over
the place. Their songs are unmanly and their ideas
seditious. They steal children. They worm their way in
everywhere. Nowadays we're quite purified of them,
but no more than a hundred years ago anyone with
dark hair had to prove he had no gypsy blood.

LANCELOT: Who told you all this about the gypsies?

CHARLEMAGNE: Our Dragon. The gypsies insolently
stood up against him in the first years of his
administration.

LANCELOT: Wonderfully independent people.

CHARLEMAGNE: Please, don't talk that way, you
mustn't.

LANCELOT: What does he eat, this Dragon of yours?

CHARLEMAGNE: Our town gives him a thousand cows,
two thousand sheep, five thousand chickens and
eighty pounds of salt a month. In summer and fall we
supplement this with another ten truck-gardens of
salad greens, asparagus and cauliflower.

LANCELOT: He's eating you out of house and home!

CHARLEMAGNE: Don't be silly! We're not complaining.
And why should we? So long as he's around, no other
dragon would dare touch us.

LANCELOT: But other dragons, I'm sure, were all exterminated long ago!

CHARLEMAGNE: But what if you're wrong? Believe me, the only way to be free and clear of dragons is to have one of your own. But that's enough of that, if you please. You'd better tell us something of interest about yourself.

LANCELOT: All right. Do you know what a Complaint Book is?

ELSA: No.

LANCELOT: Well, you're about to find out. About five years' walk from here, in the Black Mountains, there is a huge cave. And in this cave lies a book, half-filled with writing. No one lays a finger on it, yet page after page is added to what has gone before, a new one every day. Who writes in it? The world! The mountains, the grass, the rocks, the trees, the rivers see what people are doing. They are aware of all the crimes of all the criminals, all the wretchedness of those who suffer unjustly. From branch to branch, from waterdrop to waterdrop, from cloud to cloud the complaints of humanity reach that cave in the Black Mountains, and the book grows bigger. If this book did not exist, the trees would wither away with grief, and the water would turn bitter. And who is supposed to read what is written there? Me.

ELSA: You?

LANCELOT: Us. Me and a few others. We are the observant, buoyant people. We learned that there was such a book and wasted no time in finding it. He who has glanced into that book but once will find no rest until the end of time. Ah, the complaints that fill that book! But these complaints must not go unanswered. And we shall answer them.

ELSA: But how?

LANCELOT: We interfere in other people's business. We help those who must be helped. And we exterminate those who must be exterminated. Do you want help?

ELSA: How?

CHARLEMAGNE: How can you help us?

CAT: Meow!

LANCELOT: Thrice have I been mortally wounded, and each time by those whom I helped against their will. Therefore, even if you don't ask it, I shall challenge the Dragon to combat! Do you hear, Elsa?

ELSA: No, no! He'd kill you, and that would poison the last hours of my life.

CAT: Meow!

LANCELOT: I shall challenge the Dragon to single combat!

(An ever-intensifying whistling, noise-making, howling tumult resounds. The windows rattle. A fiery glow flares up outside the windows.)

CAT: Speak of the devil!

(The noise and whistling are abruptly cut off. A loud knock at the door)

CHARLEMAGNE: Come in!

(A richly attired FLUNKEY enters.)

FLUNKEY: Sir Dragon is here to see you.

CHARLEMAGNE: Be so kind as to show him in!

(The FLUNKEY flings the door wide open. Pause. The room is entered unhurriedly by a middle-aged, stocky, young-looking, tow-headed MAN, of military bearing. He sports a crewcut and a broad grin. On the whole his manner, despite

*a certain coarseness, is not devoid of a kind of amiability. He
is a bit hard of hearing.)*

MAN: Howdy, folks! Hello, Elsa, you cutie-pie! Oops,
you've got a guest. Who is he?

CHARLEMAGNE: Just a traveller, passing through.

MAN: What? Make your report loud and clear. Ten-
SHUN!

CHARLEMAGNE: He's a traveller!

MAN: Not a gypsy?

CHARLEMAGNE: Don't be silly! He's a very respectable
person.

MAN: Eh?

CHARLEMAGNE: Very respectable.

MAN: That's all right then. Hey, stranger! Why don't
you look at me? Why do you keep staring out the
door?

LANCELOT: I'm waiting for the dragon to come in.

MAN. Ha, ha! I'm the dragon.

LANCELOT: You? But I was told that you have three
heads and claws and are of enormous size!

DRAGON: I'm taking it easy today, I'm out of uniform.

CHARLEMAGNE: Sir Dragon has lived so long among
human beings that some times he turns himself into
one and drops by like an old friend.

DRAGON: Yes. We're real good friends, Charlemagne
old pal. I'm not just a friend to all of you. I'm the friend
of your childhood. What's more, I'm the friend of your
father's childhood and your grandfather's, and your
great-grandfather's. I can remember your great-great-
grandfather when he wore diapers. Hell! An unbidden
tear. Ha, ha! Lookit the bug-eyes on the stranger. You
didn't expect me to have feelings like this? Did you?

Answer me! He can't get over it, the son of a bitch.
Never mind. Forget it. Ha, ha. Elsa!

ELSA: Yes, Sir Dragon.

DRAGON: Gimme your little paw.

(ELSA *holds out her hand to the* DRAGON.)

DRAGON: You little rascal! You little trouble-maker.
What a warm little paw. Hold your kisser a little
higher! Say cheese. That's right. What you gawking at,
stranger? Eh?

LANCELOT: I'm admiring.

DRAGON: Attaboy. A smart answer. Go ahead and
admire. We're jest plain folks, stranger. Down to earth.
Have a bite to eat!

LANCELOT: No, thanks. I'm full.

DRAGON: Never mind, have some more! Why'd you
come here?

LANCELOT: On business.

DRAGON: How's that again?

LANCELOT: On business.

DRAGON: Yes, but what business? Come on, tell me.
Hey? Maybe I can help you. Why did you come here?

LANCELOT: To slay you.

DRAGON: Louder!

ELSA: No, no! He's joking! Would you like to hold my
hand again, Sir Dragon?

DRAGON: Say what?

LANCELOT: I am challenging you to single combat. Do
you hear me, Dragon!

(*The* DRAGON *turns purple but keeps silent.*)

LANCELOT: I am challenging you to single combat, for the third time. Do you hear?

(A ghastly, deafening, triple roar rings out. Despite the wall-shaking power of this roar, it is not without a certain musicality. There is nothing human about it. It is roared by the DRAGON as he clenches his fists and stamps his feet.)

DRAGON: *(Suddenly interrupting the roar. Calmly)* Fool. Well? Why don't you say something? Scared?

LANCELOT: No.

DRAGON: No?

LANCELOT: No.

DRAGON: You asked for it. *(Slightly twitches his shoulders and suddenly undergoes a startling transformation. A new head appears on the DRAGON's shoulders. The previous one disappears without a trace. An earnest, reserved man with a high forehead, a wizened face and graying blond hair stands before LANCELOT.)*

CAT: Don't be surprised, Lancelot dear. He's got three toppers. He switches them on and off as he pleases.

DRAGON: *(His voice, like his face, has changed. Quiet and dry)* Your name is Lancelot?

LANCELOT: Yes.

DRAGON: Any descendant of the famous knight errant Lancelot?

LANCELOT: We're distantly related.

DRAGON: I accept your challenge. Knights errant count as gypsies. You all have to be exterminated.

LANCELOT: I won't give up that easily.

DRAGON: To date I have exterminated: eight hundred and nine knights, nine hundred and five persons of no known profession, one old drunk, two lunatics, two women—the mother and aunt of girls I'd picked

out—one twelve-year-old boy—the brother of one
of the girls. In addition I have brought about the
extermination of six armies and five rebellious mobs.
Please be seated.

LANCELOT: *(Sits)* Thank you.

DRAGON: Do you smoke? Then go ahead, don't mind
me.

LANCELOT: Thanks. *(Takes out a pipe and unhurriedly fills
it.)*

DRAGON: Do you know which day it was I first came
into the world?

LANCELOT: An unlucky one.

DRAGON: The day of a terrible battle. That very day
Attila himself suffered defeat. —Can you conceive
how many warriors had to be laid low to accomplish
that? The earth was sodden with blood. By midnight
the leaves on the trees had turned brown. By sunrise
huge black mushrooms—the kind known as corpse-
stools—had sprung up beneath the trees. And in their
wake, from underground, crawled Yours Truly. I am
the child of War. War is what I am. The blood of dead
Huns flows in my veins,—and it is icy blood. In battle I
am icy cold, calm and deadly accurate.

(At the word "accurate", the DRAGON *makes a slight
gesture with his hand. A dry click is heard. From the
DRAGON's index finger a ribbon of flame shoots out. He
lights the tobacco in LANCELOT's now-filled pipe.)*

LANCELOT: Thank you. *(Puffs contentedly on his pipe)*

DRAGON: You oppose me. Does that mean you are
opposed to war?

LANCELOT: Don't be silly! I've been a warrior all my
life.

DRAGON: You are a stranger here, whereas the townspeople and I came to an understanding ages ago. The whole town will regard you with horror and rejoice at your death. All you have to look forward to is death with dishonor. You get my drift?

LANCELOT: No.

DRAGON: I see you're as resolute as ever?

LANCELOT: More so.

DRAGON: You are a worthy opponent.

LANCELOT: Thank you.

DRAGON: I shall take your challenge seriously.

LANCELOT: Fine.

DRAGON: Which means I'll waste no time in killing you. Right here and now.

LANCELOT: But I'm unarmed.

DRAGON: And you expect me to give you time to arm yourself? No. Didn't you just hear me say I'd take your challenge seriously? I'm launching a surprise attack, right this minute...Elsa, get a broom!

ELSA: What for?

DRAGON: I'm going to incinerate this fellow and you can sweep up his ashes.

LANCELOT: You're afraid of me?

DRAGON: I don't know the meaning of fear.

LANCELOT: Then why are you in such a hurry? Give me until tomorrow. I'll come up with a weapon and we'll meet on the field of honor.

DRAGON: Why should I?

LANCELOT: So people won't think you're a coward.

DRAGON: People will never know. These two will keep their mouths shut. You are about to die valiantly, quietly and ingloriously. *(Raises hand)*

CHARLEMAGNE: Stop!

DRAGON: Now what?

CHARLEMAGNE: You cannot kill him.

DRAGON: What's that?

CHARLEMAGNE: Now please don't fly off the handle. I'm on your side, body and soul. But, after all, I am the Keeper of Public Records.

DRAGON: What's your job got to do with it?

CHARLEMAGNE: I have in my files a treaty you signed three hundred and eighty-two years ago. This treaty has never been nullified. Please understand, I'm not objecting. I'm simply remembering. It bears the signature "Dragon".

DRAGON: So what?

CHARLEMAGNE: She is my daughter, after all. I would like her to live a little longer. That's perfectly natural.

DRAGON: Get to the point.

CHARLEMAGNE: All right, I *am* objecting—come what may. You cannot kill him. Anyone who challenges you is guaranteed safety until the day of battle, you wrote that and ratified it with an oath. And the day of battle is to be set not by you but by your challenger—that's stipulated in the treaty and sworn to. And the whole town is obligated to assist your challenger and no one will be punished for it—that's also sworn to.

DRAGON: When was this treaty negotiated?

CHARLEMAGNE: Three hundred and eighty-two years ago.

DRAGON: I had stars in my eyes in those days, a green kid with romantic ideas.

CHARLEMAGNE: But the treaty has never been nullified.

DRAGON: Big deal!...

CHARLEMAGNE: But the treaty...

DRAGON: Not another word about treaties! You're not dealing with children.

CHARLEMAGNE: But you signed it yourself, you know... I can run over and get the treaty.

DRAGON: Don't move a muscle.

CHARLEMAGNE. A man has turned up who is trying to save my little girl. Love for one's child—that's not a lot to ask. A person's entitled. And showing hospitality—a person's entitled to do that too. Why are you glaring at me like that? (*Hides his face in his hands*)

ELSA: Papa, papa!

CHARLEMAGNE: I do protest!

DRAGON: All righty. I am now going to exterminate this whole little hotbed.

LANCELOT: And the whole world will learn that you're a coward!

DRAGON: Who'll tell 'em?

(*The* CAT *leaps out the window with a single bound. He hisses from outside.*)

CAT: All, all I'll tell, to all, to all, you old newt!

(*The* DRAGON *lets out another roar, as powerful as the first, but this time hoarseness, groaning and a hacking cough are distinctly audible in it. It is the roar of an enormous, ancient and evil monster.*)

DRAGON: (*Suddenly stops roaring*) All right. The fight's on for tomorrow, as per request.

(He exits rapidly. And all at once outside the door there's whistling, booming, clattering. The walls quake, the lamp flickers, the whistling, booming and clattering die away in the distance.)

CHARLEMAGNE: He has flown away! What have I done? Oh, what have I done! I'm a damned old egotist. But what else could I do! Elsa, are you angry with me?

ELSA: No, how can you think that?

CHARLEMAGNE: Suddenly I feel so terribly weak. Excuse me. I'm going to lie down. No, no, don't come with me. Stay with our guest. Keep him entertained, he's been so kind to us. Excuse me, I'll go and lie down for a bit. *(Exits)*

(Pause)

ELSA: Why did you have to stir things up? I'm not reproaching you—but everything was all so clear and settled. There's nothing awful about dying young. Everyone else grows old, and you don't.

LANCELOT: How can you say that! Stop and think! Even trees breathe a sigh when they're chopped down.

ELSA: But I'm not complaining.

LANCELOT: And don't you feel sorry for your father?

ELSA: But, after all, he'll die whenever he wants to die. That's true happiness.

LANCELOT: And aren't you sorry to leave your friends behind?

ELSA: No. If it weren't me, the Dragon would pick one of them.

LANCELOT: But what about your betrothed?

ELSA: How did you know that I'm betrothed?

LANCELOT: Instinct. Aren't you sorry to leave your betrothed behind?

ELSA: Well, you see, the Dragon consoled Henry by making him his private secretary.

LANCELOT: Oh, so that's how things stand. In that case, of course, you aren't sorry to leave him behind. But what about your beloved town? Won't you be sorry to leave it?

ELSA: But don't you see I'm dying on behalf of my beloved town?

LANCELOT: And it accepts your sacrifice so casually?

ELSA: No, no! If I perish on Sunday, the whole town will wear mourning till Tuesday. No one will eat meat for three whole days. With their tea they'll have special muffins, called "Poor Girls" —in remembrance of me.

LANCELOT: That's all?

ELSA: What more can they do?

LANCELOT: Kill the dragon.

ELSA: That's impossible.

LANCELOT: The dragon has brainwashed you, poisoned your blood and clouded your sight. But we shall put all this to rights.

ELSA: You mustn't. If what you've said about me is true, then I'd be better off dead.

(*The* CAT *runs in.*)

CAT: Eight pussies with whom I am intimately acquainted and forty-eight of my kittens are running all over town, spreading the news of the upcoming bout. Meow! The Mayor's on his way over here.

LANCELOT: The Mayor? Splendid.

(*The* MAYOR *runs in.*)

MAYOR: Evening, Elsa. Where's the stranger?

LANCELOT: Here I am.

MAYOR: First of all, do me a favor: keep your voice down, don't gesticulate if possible, don't make any sudden moves and don't look me in the eye.

LANCELOT: Why?

MAYOR: Because my nerves are shot. I'm afflicted with all the nervous and mental illnesses in the book, not to mention three that are still unidentified. You think it's a bed of roses being Mayor under a Dragon regime?

LANCELOT: I shall slay the Dragon and everything will improve.

MAYOR: Improve? Ha-ha! Improve? Ha-ha! Improve? *(Falls in hysterics. Drinks water. Calms down)* Just daring to challenge Sir Dragon is bad enough. Everything was going fine. Sir Dragon was using his influence to put the screws on my opponent, a real crook, and his whole gang of grafters and ward-heelers. Now everything'll go to hell in a hand-basket. Sir Dragon will be so busy preparing for combat he'll neglect the town's official business and just when he was starting to take an interest.

LANCELOT: But don't you understand, you miserable wretch, I'm going to save the town?

MAYOR: The town? Ha-ha! The town! Ha-ha! *(Drinks water. Calms down)* My opponent is such a lowlife I'd sacrifice two towns to see him exterminated. Better five dragons than such scum as my opponent. Puh- leaze go away!

LANCELOT: I won't.

MAYOR: Congratulations, you've brought on a cataleptic fit. *(Freezes with a sardonic smile on his face)*

LANCELOT: But I shall save you all! Can't you understand! (MAYOR *is silent.*) Can't you understand? (MAYOR *is silent.* LANCELOT *dashes water on him.*)

MAYOR: No, I don't understand. Who asked you to fight him?

LANCELOT: The whole town is for it.

MAYOR: Oh yeah? Look out the window. The town's leading citizens have come here to beg you to beat it.

LANCELOT: Where are they?

MAYOR: Over there, cringing by the wall. Come closer, friends.

LANCELOT: Why are they tiptoeing?

MAYOR: So they won't fray my nerves. My friends, tell Lancelot what you want of him. All together now! One! Two! Three!

CHORUS OF VOICES: Get out of town! Make it snappy! Right away!

MAYOR: You see! If you're a decent, right-thinking human being, you'll hearken to the will of the people.

LANCELOT: Not on your life!

MAYOR: Congratulations, you've brought on a slight fit of insanity. *(He puts one arm akimbo, extends the other in a graceful curve.)* I'm a tea-kettle, put me on to boil!

LANCELOT: Now I understand why these poor excuses for people came on tiptoe.

MAYOR: Why?

LANCELOT: So as not to wake up the real people. I'll go and speak to them at once. *(He runs out.)*

MAYOR: Take me off, I'm boiling over! Oh well, what can he do? As soon as the Dragon gives the order, we'll throw him in jail. Elsa dear, don't get upset. When the time comes, and it's any second now, our beloved Dragon will clasp you in his embrace. Don't worry.

ELSA: I'm not worried. *(Knock at the door)* Come in.

(Enter the same FLUNKEY *who announced the* DRAGON'*s entrance.)*

MAYOR: Hello, son.

FLUNKEY: Hello, dad.

MAYOR: You got a message from him? The fight's off, right? You bring orders to lock up Lancelot?

FLUNKEY: Sir Dragon's orders are: one-- schedule the battle for tomorrow; two—provide Lancelot with arms; three—put your mind in better working order.

MAYOR: Congratulations, I've lost my mind entirely. Mind! Yoohoo! Answer me! Come out, come out, wherever you are!

FLUNKEY: My orders are to speak privately with Elsa.

MAYOR: I'm going, going, gone. *(Retreats in a hurry)*

FLUNKEY: Hello, Elsa.

ELSA: Hello, Henry.

HENRY: Are you hoping that Lancelot will save you?

ELSA: No. Are you?

HENRY: No.

ELSA: What did the Dragon order you to tell me?

HENRY: He ordered me to tell you to kill Lancelot, if it proves necessary.

ELSA: *(Appalled)* What?

HENRY: With a knife. Here it is, this jack-knife. It's poisoned...

ELSA: I won't!

HENRY: Sir Dragon ordered me to say, in that case, he will kill all your girl- friends.

ELSA: All right. Tell him I'll try.

HENRY: Sir Dragon ordered me to say, in that case, any wishy-washiness on your part will be punished as insubordination.

ELSA: I hate you!

HENRY: Sir Dragon ordered me to say, in that case, he knows how to reward faithful servants.

ELSA: Lancelot will kill your Dragon!

HENRY: Sir Dragon ordered me to say, in that case, we shall see!

(Curtain)

END OF ACT ONE

ACT TWO

*(The main square of the town. To the right, the Town
Hall with belfry where a* SENTRY *is on guard. Center an
enormous gloomy windowless brown building, with a
gigantic iron door that fills the wall from ground to roof.
On the door an inscription in Gothic letters: "Absolutely
No Entry to Human Beings." To the left, a massive ancient
fortress wall. In the middle of the square a well with
wrought-iron railings and roof.* HENRY, *out of livery and
in an apron, is polishing the bronze ornaments on the iron
door.)*

HENRY: *(Hums to the tune of* Beautiful Dreamer*)*
Beautiful Dragon remarked We shall see,
Old Draggy snarled, we shall see, we shall see,
Old Draggledy thundered, we'll see, confound me!
And we really will see! We'll see, do-re-mi!

*(*MAYOR *scurries out of the Town Hall. He's wearing a
straitjacket.)*

MAYOR: 'Morning, sonny-boy. You wanted to see me?

HENRY: 'Morning, dad. I just wanted to find out
how things are going in there. Is the meeting of the
Independent Town Council over?

MAYOR: Not a chance! Up all night and we barely
voted through today's agenda.

HENRY: Tuckered out?

MAYOR: What d'you think? In the last half hour alone I've had three changes of straitjacket. *(Yawns)* I dunno if it means rain or what, but today my damned schizophrenia is acting up something awful. Ranting and raving... Hallucinations, obsessions, you name it. *(Yawns)* Got a smoke?

HENRY: Here.

MAYOR: Get me out of this. Let's have a coffin-nail.

(HENRY unties his father. They sit side by side on the steps of the palace and start smoking.)

HENRY: When are you going to make up your mind about the weapons?

MAYOR: What weapons?

HENRY: For Lancelot.

MAYOR: What Lancelot?

HENRY: Are you crazy or something?

MAYOR: Of course. Some son you are. Completely forgot how seriously ill his poor old father is. *(Shouts)* O mortals, mortals, love your neighbor like yourself! *(Calmly)* There, you see, doesn't that sound loony?

HENRY: Never mind, dad, never mind. It'll pass.

MAYOR: I know it'll pass, but it's no fun in the meantime.

HENRY: Listen to me. I've got important news. Old Draggletail's got the jitters.

MAYOR: That's a lie!

HENRY: Oh no, it's not. Our jolly green Dragon has been flitting about all night, God knows where, regardless of the wear and tear on his wings. Didn't stagger in until sunrise. He's got that awful smell of fish he always gets when he's worried. Know what I mean?

MAYOR: Yeah, yeah.

HENRY: So this is what I managed to find out: our beloved reptilian was flitting around all night just to dig up the dirt on the famous Sir Lancelot.

MAYOR: And?

HENRY: I don't know where he's been hanging out—the Himalayas or Mount Ararat, Scotland or the Caucasus, but anyway our friend Dragnet found out that Lancelot is a professional hero. I wouldn't give the time of day to people like that. But Draggums, being a professional villain, apparently attaches some importance to them. He's been cursing a blue streak, gibbering and whining. Then the old timer got a yen for some beer. After swilling down a whole keg of his favorite brew and with nary a word of warning, the Dragon spread his webbèd wings again and so far he's been darting all over the sky like some stupid bird. Doesn't that make your flesh creep?

MAYOR: Not the least little bit.

HENRY: Daddy dear, tell me please—you're older than I am...and more experienced... What's your take on this upcoming fight? Please give me an answer. Do you think Lancelot could possibly... Give me a straight answer, none of that bureaucratic double-talk—do you think Lancelot could possibly win? Huh? Daddy dear? Answer me!

MAYOR: All right, sonny boy, I'll give you a straight answer, straight from the shoulder. You know, kid, I'd cut off my right arm for that Drag of ours! Honest to God. Just like we were flesh and blood, y'know? Why, I'd even—how can I put this? —sacrifice my life for him. Cross my heart and hope to die! No, no, no! He'll win, the son-of-a-gun! He'll win, the monstrous marvel! The scaly schemer! The flying fortress! Oh, I love him to pieces! How do I love him, let me count the ways! I love him and that's all there is to it! How's that for an answer?

HENRY: Come on, dad, won't you talk turkey, straight from the shoulder, even to your only son?

MAYOR: No way, sonny boy. You think I'm crazy? I mean, I *am* crazy, but not that crazy. I suppose the Dragon ordered you to sound me out?

HENRY: How can you, pop!

MAYOR: Attaboy, son! You did a fine job of stringing me along. I'm proud of you. Not because I'm your father, mind you. I'm proud of you because you're an expert, an old hand at this. You remember my answer?

HENRY: Of course.

MAYOR: You remember the phrases: "the monstrous marvel, the scaly schemer, the flying fortress"?

HENRY: Every last word.

MAYOR: Well, all of it should go into your report!

HENRY: Okay, pop.

MAYOR: Ah, you're my pride and joy, you're daddy's little stoolie... That's quite a nice little career you're carving out, kiddo. Need any cash?

HENRY: No, not for now, thanks anyway, pop.

MAYOR: Take it, don't be bashful...I'm loaded. I had a mild attack of kleptomania the other day. Take it...

HENRY: Thanks, but I don't need it. Now come on, tell me the truth...

MAYOR: What's eating you, sonny boy, you sound like a little kid—truth, truth, truth... After all, I'm not just any local, I'm the mayor. It's been so many years since I've told the truth—even to myself—that I've forgot what truth is. It makes me dizzy, mixes me up. Truth!

You know what the damned thing smells like? That'll do, son. Let's hear it for the Dragon! Hip, hip, hurray!

(SENTRY *on the belfry raps his halberd on the ground and shouts.*)

SENTRY: Attention! Sky dress! His Excellency has been sighted over the Gray Mountains!

(HENRY *and the* MAYOR *leap up and snap to attention, craning their heads skyward. A distant hum, which gradually dies away, can be heard.*)

SENTRY: At ease! His Excellency has turned back and is concealed by smoke and flame!

HENRY: He's patrolling.

MAYOR: Yeah, yeah. Listen, now you can answer me one little question. The Dragon really didn't give you any special orders, eh, sonny-boy?

HENRY: He did not, pop.

MAYOR: Nothing about killing him?

HENRY: Who?

MAYOR: Our savior.

HENRY: Oh, pop, pop.

MAYOR: Spit it out, sonny. Didn't he mention anything about bumping off Sir Lancelot on the sly? Don't be shy, tell me... Nothing to it... Happens every day. Eh, sonny? Not a word?

HENRY: Not a word.

MAYOR: Okay, okay, not a word. I getcha, you're under orders.

HENRY: May I remind you, Mister Mayor, that at any minute the solemn ceremony of distributing arms to Sir Hero is to take place. It's possible that Draggley intends to honor the ceremony with his presence, and you haven't got anything ready yet.

MAYOR: *(Yawns and stretches)* Okey doke, I'm on my way. We'll come up with some kind of weapons for him in nothing flat. He won't have anything to complain of. Do up my sleeves for me... Here he comes now! Here comes Lancelot!

HENRY: Get him out of here! Elsa may show up any minute and I have things to discuss with her.

(LANCELOT enters.)

MAYOR: *(Hysterically)* Honor and glory unto thee, hosanna in the highest, George the Dragon-slayer! Oops, my mistake, in my delirium I took you for him. There's a wonderful resemblance.

LANCELOT: Quite possibly. He is a distant relative of mine.

MAYOR: And how did you while away the night?

LANCELOT: I walked around.

MAYOR: Make friends with anybody?

LANCELOT: Of course.

MAYOR: Who with?

LANCELOT: The panic-stricken citizens of your town sicked their dogs on me. But your dogs are very level-headed. So I made friends with them. They understood me, because they love their masters and wish them well. We chewed the fat till dawn.

MAYOR: Catch any fleas?

LANCELOT: No. They were sleek, well-groomed hounds.

MAYOR: You happen to remember their names?

LANCELOT: They asked me not to say.

MAYOR: I can't stand dogs.

LANCELOT: Tough luck.

MAYOR: Too uncomplicated.

LANCELOT: You think it's so easy to love human beings? Listen, dogs know only too well what sort of people their masters are. They weep for them but they love them. They're the real workers. You sent for me?

MAYOR: For-me-dable! They're writing songs of love but not for me. The bells of hell go ting-a-ling-a-ling for you but not for me. To make a long story short, I did send for you, Sir Lancelot.

LANCELOT: How can I serve you?

MAYOR: They also serve who only stand and wait. Fifth floor: women's wear, modesty and see-through dresses. Shoes, ships, sealing wax, cabbages and kings. One flew east and one flew west and one flew over the cuckoo's nest. The Independent Town Council is waiting for you, Sir Lancelot.

LANCELOT: Why?

MAYOR: Why o why o why o, why did I ever leave— my home, home on the range. Why beat about the bush when you'd bravely buss a beauty? Why buss a beauty when the burly brawl's beginning? The members of the Independent Town Council have to see you in person to determine just what sort of weapons suit you best, Sir Lancelot. Come on, let'em take a look at you!

(LANCELOT and MAYOR leave.)

HENRY: Beautiful Dragon said, we shall see; Old Draggles snarled, we shall see, we shall see; Old Draggler remarked, we'll see, confound me,—And we really will see!

(Enter ELSA.)

HENRY: Elsa!

ELSA: Yes. You sent for me?

HENRY: I did. What a pity there's a sentry posted on the tower. If it weren't for that most annoying impediment, I would take you in my arms and kiss you.

ELSA: And I would slap your face.

HENRY: Oh, Elsa, Elsa! You always were a bit too prim and proper. But on you it looked good. There was something lurking underneath your modesty. Dragdad's got a nose for the girls. He's always picked out the really promising ones, the frisky old rascal. Hasn't Lancelot made a pass at you yet?

ELSA: Shut up.

HENRY: But of course he wouldn't. Even if you were only an old bag, he'd stick his neck out and fight. A lot he cares who he saves. That's part of his training. He hasn't even taken a good look at you yet.

ELSA: We've only just met.

HENRY: That's no excuse.

ELSA: You had me brought here just to tell me that?

HENRY: Oh no. I had you brought here to ask you to marry me.

ELSA: Stop!

HENRY: No kidding. I am empowered to convey the following information: if you are compliant and kill Lancelot, if the need arises, then as a reward Dragon will let you go.

ELSA: I won't.

HENRY: Let me finish. To replace you he will choose another girl, no one you know, a member of the lower classes. She was next on the list anyway. Take your pick—a pointless death or a life filled with delights you've only dreamed of, and then so rarely it's a shame.

ELSA: He's getting scared!

HENRY: Who? Draggletail? I know all his shortcomings. Call him what you like: a little Caesar, a loudmouth, a parasite—but he's no coward.

ELSA: Yesterday he was issuing threats, today he's making deals.

HENRY: I talked him into it.

ELSA: You?

HENRY: I'm the real Dragon-killer, I'll have you know. I can twist him round my little finger. I waited for the right moment—and it was worth the wait. I'm not such a fool that I'd hand you over to just anybody.

ELSA: I don't believe you.

HENRY: Yes you do.

ELSA: It doesn't matter, I can't kill anyone!

HENRY: But you're carrying the knife all the same. There it is, dangling from your belt. I've got to go, dearest. I have to put on my full-dress uniform. But I leave with a load off my mind. You'll carry out your orders for your sake and mine. Think it over! Life, a whole life ahead of us—if you make the right choice. Think it over, you fascinating creature. (*Exits*)

ELSA: My God! My cheeks are scorching as if I'd kissed him. What a disgrace! He almost talked me into it... Which means I'm that sort of person!...All right then. A good thing too. I'm fed up with this! I was the most submissive girl in town. I trusted everyone. And where did it get me? Oh yes, everyone respected me, but they had all the happiness. Now they're sitting at home, choosing their fanciest dresses, ironing their ruffles. Curling their hair. Getting ready to come and stare at my misfortune. I can just see them powdering their faces in the mirror, saying, "Poor Elsa, poor girl,

she was so sweet!" And alone in all the town, I, all
by myself, stand in the square and eat my heart out.
And that idiot sentry bugs his eyes at me, as he thinks
about what the dragon is going to do to me today. And
tomorrow that soldier will be alive, resting after his
stint on duty. He'll take a stroll to the waterfall where
the river is so sprightly that even the most miserable
people smile when they see how brilliantly it splashes.
Or he'll go to the park where the gardener grows such
wonderful pansies with eyes that wink and blink and
even know how to read, so long as the letters are big
and the story has a happy ending. Or he'll go for a row
on the lake, the one the dragon once set a-boiling and
where the water-nymphs have been so subdued ever
since. They don't even drown people any more, they
just sit in a shallow spot selling life-belts. But they're as
beautiful as ever and the soldiers love to chat them up.
And that stupid sentry will tell the water- nymphs how
merrily the music played, how everybody wept, when
the Dragon carried me off. And the water-nymphs will
start moaning and groaning, "Oh, poor Elsa, oh, poor
girl, such lovely weather today and she's not around
to see it." I won't have it! I want to see it all, hear it all,
feel it all. So there! I brought the knife to kill myself.
But I won't. So there!

(LANCELOT *emerges from the Town Hall.*)

LANCELOT: Elsa! What luck to run into you!

ELSA: Why?

LANCELOT: Ah, my beauteous maiden, today is a weary
one for me, my soul craves respite, if but for a brief
moment. And now, what a coincidence, I run into you.

ELSA: You were at the council meeting?

LANCELOT: I was.

ELSA: Why did they summon you?

LANCELOT: They offered me money to give up the fight.

ELSA: And what did you reply?

LANCELOT: I replied: you poor fools! Let's not talk
about them, Elsa, you're even lovelier today than you
were yesterday. It's a true sign that I am fond of you.
Do you believe that I will rescue you?

ELSA: No.

LANCELOT: I'm not offended. That's how much I like
you, I suppose.

(ELSA's GIRL-FRIENDS *run in.*)

FIRST GIRL-FRIEND: Here we are!

SECOND GIRL-FRIEND: We're Elsa's very best friends.

THIRD GIRL-FRIEND: We've been soulmates ever so
many years, since we were children.

FIRST GIRL-FRIEND: She was the smartest of us all.

SECOND GIRL-FRIEND: She was the sweetest of us all.

THIRD GIRL-FRIEND: And even so she loved us more
than anybody. She would do the sewing, if only you
asked her, and help you with your homework, and
would comfort you when you thought you were the
most unhappy girl on earth.

FIRST GIRL-FRIEND: Are we late?

SECOND GIRL-FRIEND: You're really going to fight him?

THIRD GIRL-FRIEND: Sir Lancelot, could you get us up
on the roof of the town hall? They won't say no if you
ask them. We do so want to get the best view of the
fight.

FIRST GIRL-FRIEND: Oh look, now you're getting cross.

SECOND GIRL-FRIEND: And you won't talk to us.

THIRD GIRL-FRIEND: But we're not such bad girls after
all.

FIRST GIRL-FRIEND: You think we're deliberately keeping you from saying good-bye to Elsa.

SECOND GIRL-FRIEND: But it's not on purpose.

THIRD GIRL-FRIEND: Henry ordered us not to leave you two alone together, until Sir Dragon gives permission.

FIRST GIRL-FRIEND: He ordered us to chatter...

SECOND GIRL-FRIEND: So here we are, chattering away like idiots...

THIRD GIRL-FRIEND: Because otherwise we'd be weeping. And you're just passing through and can't imagine how embarrassing it is to cry in front of strangers.

(CHARLEMAGNE *emerges from the Town Hall.*)

CHARLEMAGNE: The meeting is adjourned, Sir Lancelot. A resolution concerning your weapons has been passed. Forgive us. Have pity on us poor murderers, Sir Lancelot.

(*Trumpets sound a fanfare. From the Town Hall come* SERVANTS *who roll out carpets and set up armchairs. They stand a large, sumptuously decorated chair in the middle. To the right and left, simpler chairs. Enter the* MAYOR, *surrounded by the members of the Town Council. He is in high spirits.* HENRY, *wearing full-dress livery, is with them.*)

MAYOR: That's a real knee-slapper... How does it go? "Sometimes I take it out of my mouth?" Ha ha ha! Say, have you heard this one? This is great. A gypsy, a Jew and a queer got arrested...

(*Trumpets sound a fanfare*)

MAYOR: Ah, it's all ready already...Okay, remind me to tell it to you after the ceremony...Take your places, gentlemen. We'll be done with this in a jiffy.

(The members of the Town Council stand to the right and left of the armchair in the center. HENRY *stands behind the chair-back.)*

MAYOR: *(Bows to the empty chair. Rapid staccato.)* Deeply moved and totally bowled over by the trust you've invested in us, Your Excellency, by allowing us to make such an important decision, we request you to take the place of honor. Requesting once, requesting twice, requesting thrice. It breaks my heart, but what're y'gonna do—we'll have to start without him. Take your seats, gentlemen. The meeting is cuckold... *(Pause)* Water!

*(*SERVANT *gets water from the well.* MAYOR *drinks.)*

MAYOR: The meeting is scalded... Water! *(Drinks. Clears his throat. In falsetto)* The meeting *(In a deep bass)* is called to... Water! *(Drinks. Falsetto)* Thank you, darling! *(Bass)* Get outa here, you creep! *(In his own voice.)* Congratulations, gentlemen, my split personality has arrived. *(Bass)* What are you up to, you dizzy bitch? *(Falsetto)* Can't you see I'm chairing a meeting. *(Bass)* Since when is that woman's work? *(Falsetto)* You think I asked for this, sweeetheart? No cracks about my gender when I'm about to read the agenda. *(In his own voice)* Moved: that we supply a certain Lancelot with weapons. Resolved: to do so, but under duress. Hey you! Bring in the weapons!

(Trumpets sound a fanfare. Enter SERVANTS. *The* FIRST SERVANT *gives* LANCELOT *a brass cuspidor with a leather chinstrap attached.)*

LANCELOT: This is a spitoon.

MAYOR: True, but it's been commissioned to serve as your helmet. And this metal ashtray has been conscripted as your shield. Don't worry. In our town even inanimate objects are well disciplined and obedient. They'll carry out their duties conscientiously.

Unfortunately we're clean out of suits of armor. But
we do have a lance. *(Hands* LANCELOT *a sheet of paper)*
This certificate, signed and sealed, states that the lance
is presently being repaired. Just you present this to
Sir Dragon during the battle and all's well that ends
well. Now you're set. *(Bass)* Adjourn the meeting, you
dizzy broad! *(Falsetto)* I'm doing it, I'm doing it, damn
it. There's no cause for you to get in such a snit. *(Sings)*
One, two, three, four, A knight went forth to fight a
war... *(Bass)* End the meeting, for Chrissake! *(Falsetto)*
What do you think I'm doing? *(Sings)* Old Dragnet
dropped down from the sky And shot the knight
smack in the eye... Pow-kazow, ouch-ouch-ouch, this
mating is adjourned.

SENTRY: Attention! Sky dress! His Excellency has been
sighted over the Gray Mountains and is flying this way
with terrific speed.

*(Everyone leaps up and freezes in place, their heads tilted
skywards. A distant hum, which grows with terrifying
rapidity. The stage darkens. Total darkness. The hum is cut
short.)*

SENTRY: Attention! His Excellency, like a storm cloud,
is hovering overhead, blocking out the sun. Hold your
breath!

(Two greenish flares flash out.)

CAT: *(In a whisper)* Lancelot, it's me, the Cat.

LANCELOT: *(In a whisper)* I recognized you at once, by
your eyes.

CAT: I'll be dozing on the fortress wall. Take a moment,
pay me a call and I'll purr something very pleasant to
you.

SENTRY: Attention! His Excellency is diving head first
to the square.

(Deafening whistle and roar. Lights flash. In the big armchair a puny, deathly pale, elderly little man with his feet up.)

CAT: *(From the fortress wall)* Don't be frightened, Lancelot dear. That's his third topper. He changes them whenever he likes.

MAYOR: Your Excellency! In the independent municipality entrusted to me nothing has occurred. Jailed: one individual. Present...

DRAGON: *(Very quietly, in a cracked tenor voice)* Get out! Everybody out: except the stranger.

(Everyone leaves. Left on stage are CAT, DRAGON and LANCELOT. CAT dozes on the fortress wall, curled into a ball.)

DRAGON: How's your health?

LANCELOT: Excellent, thanks.

DRAGON: What's that crockery on the ground?

LANCELOT: My weapons.

DRAGON: That's what my people came up with?

LANCELOT. Yes.

DRAGON: The bastards. Offended perhaps?

LANCELOT: No.

DRAGON: Bragging. My blood runs cold, but even I would be offended. Scared?

LANCELOT: No.

DRAGON: Bragging, bragging. My people are very scary. You won't find their like anywhere else. My doing. Cut to my pattern.

LANCELOT: But people nevertheless.

DRAGON: On the outside.

LANCELOT: No.

DRAGON: If you were to see their souls—ugh, you'd tremble all over.

LANCELOT: No.

DRAGON: You'd even run away. You wouldn't die for such cripples. I personally crippled them, my dear boy. I crippled them good and proper. Human souls, dear boy, are very resilient. Chop the body in half—a man kicks the bucket. But chop up the soul—and he just knuckles under. No, no, you won't find souls like these anywhere else. Only in my town. Armless souls, legless souls, deaf-mute souls, shackled souls, stool-pigeon souls, souls damned to hell. You know why the Mayor pretends to be crazy? To hide the fact that he has no soul at all. Bed-wetting souls, money-grubbing souls, charred souls, dead souls. No, no, it's a pity they're invisible.

LANCELOT: Lucky for you.

DRAGON: Why so?

LANCELOT: People would be terrified to see with their own eyes how their souls have been deformed. They would die the death rather than remain enslaved. Then who would feed you?

DRAGON: Who the hell knows, you may be right. All right, shall we begin?

LANCELOT: Go to it.

DRAGON: First say farewell to the girl for whose sake you're dying. Hey, boy!

(HENRY runs in.)

DRAGON: Fetch Elsa!

(HENRY runs out.)

DRAGON: You like the girl I've picked out?

LANCELOT: I like her very, very much.

DRAGON: Glad to hear it. I like her very, very much. An outstanding girl. Submissive girl.

(Enter ELSA *and* HENRY.*)*

DRAGON: Come here, come, my dear. Look me in the eyes. That's right. Very nice. Bright little eyes. You may kiss my hand. That's right. Lovely. Warm lips. Which means, your soul is calm. You want to say good-bye to Sir Lancelot?

ELSA: Whatever you order, Sir Dragon.

DRAGON: Well, that's what I order. Go on. Speak tenderly to him. *(Quietly)* Ever so, ever so tenderly speak to him. Kiss him farewell. Never mind, I'll be here. You may do in my presence. And then kill him. Never mind, never mind. I'll be here. You'll do it in my presence. Go ahead. You may walk a little farther with him. After all, my eyesight's twenty-twenty. I shall see it all. Go ahead.

*(*ELSA *walks over to* LANCELOT.*)*

ELSA: Sir Lancelot, I have been ordered to say good-bye to you.

LANCELOT: Good, Elsa. Let's say good-bye, just in case. This will be a fight to the finish. Anything can happen. At parting I want to tell you that I love you, Elsa.

ELSA: Me!

LANCELOT: Yes, Elsa. Even yesterday I was fond of you when I glimpsed you through the window and saw how calmly you were walking home with your father. Then I saw how every time we met, you looked more beautiful. Aha, I thought. So that's it. Then, when you kissed the Dragon's paw, I didn't get indignant. I was simply terribly hurt. And suddenly it became clear to me, I love you, Elsa. Don't be angry. I wanted terribly for you to know.

ELSA: I thought you would have challenged the Dragon whoever was involved. Even if another girl had been in my place.

LANCELOT: Of course I would have. I can't stand them, dragons, that is. But for your sake I'm ready to strangle him with my bare hands, revolting though it would be.

ELSA: In other words, you love me?

LANCELOT: Very much. It terrifies me to think of! If, yesterday, at the crossroads, I had turned right or left, we might never have met. Frightening thought, isn't it?

ELSA: Yes.

LANCELOT: Terrifying to think of. It occurs to me that there is no one in the world closer to me than you are, and I consider your town mine, because you live here. If I...well, I mean, if we don't manage to meet again, don't ever forget me.

ELSA: No.

LANCELOT: Don't ever forget. Why, just now, for the first time this blessed day, you've looked me in the face. And your eyes shot me through with warmth, as if you had caressed me. I'm a wanderer, a buoyant cork, but all my life has been spent fighting tough battles. Here a dragon, there cannibals, another place giants. Never a dull moment... Arduous, thankless work. And yet I was always happy. I never got tired. And I've often fallen in love.

ELSA: Often?

LANCELOT: Of course. You wander far and wide, getting into fights and meeting girls. They're forever getting kidnapped by bandits or bagged by giants or ending up in cannibal kitchens. And these villains always pick out the best girls—especially the cannibals. So you fall in love, usually. But was it like this? It was just a game with the others. I laughed at them. But you,

Elsa, if we were alone now, I'd cover you with kisses. Honest. And I'd carry you away from here. We two would bestride forests and mountains. It's not as hard as all that. No, I would get you a steed with such a saddle that you would never grow weary. And I would walk by your stirrup and feast my eyes on you. And no man would dare to insult you.

(ELSA *takes* LANCELOT *by the hand.*)

DRAGON: Attagirl. She's got him well in hand.

HENRY: Yes. She's nobody's fool, Your Excellency.

LANCELOT: Elsa, you look as if you were about to cry?

ELSA: I am.

LANCELOT: Why?

ELSA: Because I feel sorry.

LANCELOT: For whom?

ELSA: Myself and you. There'll be no happiness for either of us, Sir Lancelot. Why was I born into the world under the Dragon?

LANCELOT: Elsa, I always tell the truth. We shall be happy. Trust me.

ELSA: Oh, oh, don't.

LANCELOT: You and I shall tread the forest path, merry and happy. Just you and I.

ELSA: No, no, don't.

LANCELOT: And the sky above us will be sunny. No one will dare to swoop down on us out of it.

ELSA: Truly?

LANCELOT: Truly. Oh, do they know in your poor town how people can love one another? The fear, fatigue, mistrust in you will be consumed, will disappear forever, that's how much I'll love you. And you will fall asleep with a smile on your lips and wake up with a smile on your lips and call to me—that's how much you will love me. And you'll love yourself as well. You will walk proudly and peacefully. You will realize, whenever I kiss you, what a fine person you are. And the trees in the forest will speak lovingly to us, and the birds and the beasts, because true lovers understand everything and are at one with the whole world. And everyone will be happy for us, because true lovers bring good luck.

DRAGON: What's he droning on about over there?

HENRY: He's preaching. Learning is light and ignorance is darkness. Wash your hands before meals. Etcetera. Boring old stuff...

DRAGON: Aha, aha. She's put her hand on his shoulder! Attagirl.

ELSA: Even if we do not live to see such happiness. Even so, yes, even so I'm happy now. These monsters are spying on us. But we have travelled far away, to Wonderland. No one has ever spoken this way to me, my dear. I never knew that the world held such persons as you. Even yesterday I was still as submissive as a dog and dared not think about you. And yet at night I quietly slipped downstairs and drank the wine you left in your glass. Only now do I realize that this was my way of kissing you by night, ever so secretly, for being my champion. You don't realize how confused our feelings are, we poor, browbeaten girls. Not long ago I thought I hated you. But that was my way of falling in love with you, ever so secretly. My dearest! I love you—what a joy to say it out loud. And what a joy to... (*Kisses* LANCELOT)

DRAGON: (*Stamping with impatience*) Now she'll do it, now she'll do it, now she'll do it!

ELSA: And now let me go, dear. *(Frees herself from*
LANCELOT*'s embrace. Draws the knife from its sheath.)* You
see this knife? The Dragon ordered me to kill you with
this knife. Look!

DRAGON: Now! Now! Now!

HENRY: Do it, do it!

(ELSA throws the dagger down the well.)

HENRY: The contemptible slut!

DRAGON: *(Roars)* How dare you!...

ELSA: Not another word! What makes you think I'll let
you swear and curse now that he has kissed me? I love
him. And he will slay you.

LANCELOT: That's the plain truth, Sir Dragon.

DRAGON: Izzat so? Never mind. I'll have to fight.
(Yawns) To tell the truth, I'm not sorry for it, I recently
worked out an interesting manoeuvre with Paw N
moving in direction X. Now I can try it out on a real
body. Orderly, assemble the guard.

(HENRY runs out.)

DRAGON: Go home, you little fool, and after the fight
we'll have a nice heart-to-heart about the whole matter.

(Enter HENRY with the guard.)

DRAGON: Listen, guards, I had something to tell you...
Oh yes... Escort this young lady home and keep close
watch over her.

(LANCELOT takes a step forward.)

ELSA. Don't. Save your strength. When you've slain
him, come to me, I shall wait for you and tell over
every word you spoke to me today. I believe in you.

LANCELOT: I shall come for you.

DRAGON: That's enough of that. Go away.

(The guards escort ELSA *out.)*

DRAGON: Boy, remove the sentry from the belfry and put him in prison. Tonight we'll have to chop off his head. He heard how that slut shouted at me, and he might gossip about it in the barracks. Deal with it. Then come and smear my claws with poison.

*(*HENRY *runs out.)*

DRAGON: *(To* LANCELOT*)* And you stay right here, you hear? And wait. I'm not saying when I'll begin. Real warfare always starts unexpectedly. Get me?

(Crawls off the chair and exits into the palace. LANCELOT *goes over to the* CAT.*)*

LANCELOT: Well, cat, what was that something pleasant you were going to purr to me?

CAT: Take a look to your right, Lancelot dear. In the middle of that cloud of dust is a donkey. Kicking up his heels. Five men are arguing with the stubborn mule. Now I'll sing him a little song. *(Meows)* You see how the stubborn mule is springing towards us. But he's going to be obstinate again by that wall, and you can talk to the teamsters who drive him. There they are.

(Behind the wall appears the head of a DONKEY, *which stops in a cloud of dust. Five* TEAMSTERS *shout at it.* HENRY *runs across the square.)*

HENRY: *(To the* TEAMSTERS*)* What are you doing here?

TWO TEAMSTERS: *(In unison)* Taking goods to market, boss.

HENRY: What sort?

TWO TEAMSTERS: Carpets, boss.

HENRY: Move it, move it. You're not allowed to loiter around the palace!

TWO TEAMSTERS: This donkey's stubborn as a mule, boss.

DRAGON: *(Off)* Boy!

HENRY: Move it, move it! *(Runs into the palace.)*

TWO TEAMSTERS: *(In unison)* Good morning, Sir Lancelot. We're on your side, Sir Lancelot. *(Clear their throats in unison)* Heh-hem. Don't get the wrong idea if we talk in unison—we been workin' side-by-side since we was boys, workin' so hand-in-glove that we think and talk like one person. We even fell in love on the same day at the same time and married twin sisters who was related. We've wove an awful lot of carpets in our day but never better than the one we worked on last night, for you. *(They remove a carpet from the donkey's back and spread it on the ground.)*

LANCELOT: What a beautiful carpet!

TWO TEAMSTERS: You bet. Best quality carpet, double pile, wool and silk blend, and colors dyed accordin' to our special secret process. But the carpet's surprise ain't in the wool or the silk or the dyes. *(Sotto voce)* It's a flyin' carpet.

LANCELOT: Marvelous! Quickly, tell me how to drive it.

TWO TEAMSTERS: Easy as pie, Sir Lancelot. This here corner with the sun wove in it is for gainin' altitude. This here corner with the globe wove in it is for losin' altitude. This here corner with the swallows wove in it is for stunt flyin'. And this here corner's for dragons. Bend it up—and you'll go into a nose-dive right at your enemy's noggin. Here we wove in a jug of wine and a tasty snack. Smite and kill and eat your fill. No, no. Don't thank us. Our great-granddaddies never stopped lookin' down the road, waitin' for you to show up. Our granddaddies waited too. So did we—and you showed up.

(They leave quickly and immediately the THIRD TEAMSTER
runs up to LANCELOT *with a cardboard hatbox.)*

THIRD TEAMSTER: Top of the morning to you, my dear
sir! Will you allow me? May I see your right profile.
And now the other one. Excellent. Sir, I am a master
hatter and maker of headgear. I confect the finest hats
and caps in existence. I've got quite a reputation in this
town. Every dog here knows me.

CAT: And cat as well.

THIRD TEAMSTER: There, you see! Without taking a
single measurement, merely by a sharp glance at the
customer, I can create a finished product that is most
flattering to people, and that makes my day. There's
one lady, for instance, whose husband makes love to
her only when she's wearing a hat I've styled. She even
wears it to bed and tells everyone that she's a happy
woman, thanks to me. I was up all last night working
for you, sir, and I cried like a baby, it was so sad.

LANCELOT: What was?

THIRD TEAMSTER: There's something really tragic
about this particular style. It's a cap of invisibility.

LANCELOT: Marvelous!

THIRD TEAMSTER: The minute you put it on you
vanish, and the poor hatter never knows if it suits you
or not. Take it, but don't try it on while I'm around. I
couldn't stand it! I just couldn't stand it!

(He runs off. Immediately a FOURTH TEAMSTER *walks up to*
LANCELOT—*a bearded, surly fellow with a pack on his back.*
He opens the pack and takes out a sword and a lance.)

FOURTH TEAMSTER: There. Hammered overtime. Good
luck.

(Exits. A FIFTH TEAMSTER *runs up to* LANCELOT—*a gray-*
haired little coot holding a stringed instrument.)

FIFTH TEAMSTER: I'm a specialist in hand-crafting musical instruments, Sir Lancelot. My great-great-great-granddad started work on this little wonder. We've kept at it from generation to generation, and in going through so many human hands, it's turned into a regular human being. It'll be your faithful companion in battle. Your hands may be busy with sword and lance but it can take care of itself. It'll work like a tuning fork and keep itself in tune. It'll replace its own broken strings and give itself the downbeat. It'll play an encore, if that's what's called for, or clam up, if that's what's called for. Ain't that so?

(The musical instrument replies with a musical phrase.)

FIFTH TEAMSTER: You see? We heard tell, all of us, how you were wandering up and down the town on your lonesome, and we pushed to make sure you were armed from top to toe. We've been waiting and waiting for a hundred years. The dragon kept us muzzled, so we waited with muzzles on. And now the waiting's over. Kill him and set us free. Ain't that so?

(The musical instrument replies with a musical phrase. The FIFTH TEAMSTER *bows himself out.)*

CAT: When the fight starts, we—the donkey and I—plan to hide in the barn back of the palace, so my fur won't get singed by a stray flame. If you need anything, give us a shout. In his saddle-bags the donkey's got alcoholic beverages, cherry turnovers, a whetstone for the sword, spare blades for the lance, needles and thread.

LANCELOT: Thanks. *(Stands on the carpet. Takes up the weapons, places the musical instrument at his feet. Picks up the cap of invisibility, dons it and disappears.)*

CAT: Exquisite workmanship. First-rate craftsmen. You still here, Lancelot dear?

LANCELOT: *(Off)* No. I'm climbing steadily. See you later, friends.

CAT: See you later, my dear. Goodness, what a lot of fuss and feathers. No, despair is a much, much nicer state of affairs. You snooze and stop expecting anything to change. Am I right, Donkeykins?

(The DONKEY *waggles his ears.)* I'm not conversant with ear language. So let's talk with words, Donkeykins. We're not very well acquainted, but since we're working together, we might as well have a friendly meow. It's agony when you're waiting and there's no one to talk to. So do let's have a meow.

DONKEY: I don't hold with meowing.

CAT: Well, then let's talk human. The dragon thinks Lancelot is still here, but his scent's gone cold. Isn't that a scream?

DONKEY: *(Gloomily)* Hilarious.

CAT: Then why aren't you laughing?

DONKEY: And get a beating. The minute I laugh out loud, folks say: There's that goddam donkey braying again. And they give me hell.

CAT: So that's it! You must have quite a piercing laugh?

DONKEY: Uh-huh.

CAT: And what do you laugh at?

DONKEY: Depends...I'll be thinking and thinking and then I'll remember something funny. Like horses. Very funny.

CAT: Why?

DONKEY: No reason... The dopes.

CAT: Do forgive me if I seem inquisitive. But there's something I've wanted to ask you for the longest time...

DONKEY: What?

CAT: How can you eat thistles?

DONKEY: Why not?

CAT. Of course one does run across some succulent stems in the high grass. But thistles...they're so dry!

DONKEY: So what. I got a taste for prickly.

CAT: What about meat?

DONKEY: What about meat?

CAT: Ever tried to eat it?

DONKEY: Meat's not food. Meat's cargo. It's for loading in my wagon, you dimwit.

CAT: What about milk?

DONKEY: Well, okay, I did drink it when I was a kid.

CAT: Glory be, something nice and soothing to chat about.

DONKEY: True. Nice to remember. Soothing. Mother's kind. Milk's warm. Suck and suck and suck. Heaven! Delicious.

CAT: Milk's nice to lap up too.

DONKEY: I don't hold with lapping.

CAT: *(Leaps up)* Hear that?

DONKEY: He's stamping his hooves, the slimy creep.

(A triple howl from the DRAGON*)*

DRAGON: Lancelot! Feast your eyes on me before the battle. Where are you?

*(*HENRY *runs into the square. Rushes around looking for* LANCELOT, *looks down well.)*

DRAGON: Where is he?

HENRY: In hiding, Your Excellency.

DRAGON: Hey, Lancelot! Where are you?! *(Clang of sword)* Who dares to strike me?

LANCELOT: *(Off)* 'Tis I, Lancelot!

(Total darkness. A menacing roar. A flash of light. HENRY *rushes into the Town Hall. Din of battle.)*

CAT: Let's take cover.

DONKEY: High time.

(They run off. The square fills with people. The people are preternaturally quiet. They whisper back and forth as they watch the sky.)

FIRST CITIZEN:
It gets on my nerves how they drag out this fight.

SECOND CITIZEN:
Two minutes it's lasted and no end in sight.

FIRST CITIZEN:
I hope that it's over and done with real quick.

SECOND CITIZEN:
Oh dear, now it's lunchtime and I feel too sick
To eat lunch. Things were nice and serene.
This is awful! Look, the Gardener's come on the scene.
Good day, why do you look so down in the dumps?

GARDENER:
Today all my roses have blossomed in clumps—
Tea roses, bread roses, wine roses, each variety:
Take one look, you get drunk and you belch with
satiety.
Sir Dragon had promised to drop by today:
If he liked what he saw he would foot the outlay
For further research.
Now I'm left in the lurch
While he goes off to war.
What the hell's it all for?
War's a ruin to science; all it can do is spoil it,
And the fruits of my labor will go down the toilet.

PEDDLER: *(In a brisk whisper)*
Who'll buy, who'll buy, who'll buy, who'll buy?
Smoked glasses on offer—just step up and try!
Once on your nose, you'll see it's no joke—
Viewed this way the dragon will go up in smoke.

(Everyone laughs quietly.)

FIRST CITIZEN: Ha ha, what a risky thing to say to folk!

SECOND CITIZEN:
Imagine, the dragon will go up in smoke!

(People buy glasses.)

LITTLE BOY: Momma, momma, look at the sky!
The dragon's on the run!
Who's chasing him up there so high?

EVERYONE: Ssshhh!

FIRST CITIZEN: Little boy, it's all in fun.
These are the dragon's tactics.

LITTLE BOY: Well, his ticktacks look so strange.
Why's he got his tail between his legs
Like a mongrel with the mange?

EVERYONE: Ssshhh!

FIRST CITIZEN: Little boy, his tail's between his legs
According to a plan.

FIRST FEMALE CITIZEN: Six minutes now the war's gone
on, and stop it no one can.
No end in sight, the world's a mess, we're all in a bad
mood,
And three times now the shopkeepers have raised the
price of food.

SECOND FEMALE CITIZEN:
Raising prices is normal, that story is old.
What I saw on my way here will make blood run cold.
Such staples as coffee and sugar and cream
Had vanished, the shelves were all empty and clean.

Such products are nervous, they said, and the threat
Of war is enough to make any cheese sweat.
So foodstuffs, when faced with a dire situation,
Are always the first named for evacuation.

(Cries of indignation. The crowd shies away to one side.
CHARLEMAGNE *appears.)*

CHARLEMAGNE: Good day, friends! *(Silence)* Don't you
know me?

FIRST CITIZEN: Certainly not. Since last night you've
become a total stranger.

CHARLEMAGNE: Why?

GARDENER: Awful people. Letting in strangers. Riling
the dragon's temper. It's worse than walking on the
grass. And then they got the nerve to ask why.

SECOND CITIZEN: Personally I stopped talking to you
the minute your house was put under martial law.

CHARLEMAGNE: Yes, that's awful, isn't it? Those stupid
guards won't let me in to see my own daughter. They
say the Dragon gave orders not to let anyone in to see
Elsa.

FIRST CITIZEN: So what. From their standpoint they're
absolutely right.

CHARLEMAGNE: Elsa's all alone in there. True, she
nodded to me very cheerfully out the window, but that
was probably just to reassure me. Oh dear, wherever I
go, I'm out of place.

SECOND CITIZEN: What do you mean, out of place? You
mean you were fired from your job as Keeper of the
Records?

CHARLEMAGNE: No.

SECOND CITIZEN: Then what are you talking about?

CHARLEMAGNE: You really fail to understand me?

FIRST CITIZEN: Not at all. But ever since you got so chummy with that outside agitator, we don't speak the same language.

(Din of battle, clang of swords)

LITTLE BOY: *(Pointing at sky)*
Momma, momma! Look at the sky!
The dragon has turned upside-down!
Somebody's making sparks to fly
By hitting him all around.

EVERYONE: Ssshhh!

(Trumpets sound. Enter HENRY *and the* MAYOR.*)*

MAYOR: Hear ye, hear ye! To prevent an outbreak of eye-strain and for no other reason, no one is permitted to look up at the sky. All aerial events will be reported in an official bulletin to be broadcast by Sir Dragon's private secretary, if it should ever become necessary.

FIRST CITIZEN: The proper thing to do.

SECOND CITIZEN: High time too.

LITTLE BOY: Momma, momma, why oh why
Will it hurt us to watch him
Beat up in the sky?

EVERYONE: Ssshhh!

*(*ELSA's GIRL-FRIENDS *show up.)*

FIRST GIRL-FRIEND:
Ten minutes, ten minutes, will this war never end?
Why won't Lancelot sound the retreat?

SECOND GIRL-FRIEND:
He knows the dragon can't be beat.

THIRD GIRL-FRIEND:
He does it on purpose to send us round the bend.

FIRST GIRL-FRIEND:
I left my gloves at Elsa's, but I don't care.

My very best pair, but I don't care.
The war has made me tired and sick,
I can't be bothered to care a tick.
I just don't care!

SECOND GIRL-FRIEND:
No matter what, I'm numb to it, and I don't care.
Those brand-new pumps of Elsa's, I don't care.
She wanted me her pumps to wear
As a keepsake, but I left them there.
(And do I give them a moment's thought?)
No, I don't care!

THIRD GIRL-FRIEND:
That stranger mixed in our affairs, but I don't care.
If not for him, think we'd be where—but, I don't care.
Elsa would be the Dragon's prey,
And we'd be weeping "Well-a-day!"
(And doing it prettily too!)
But I don't care.

PEDDLER: *(In a brisk whisper)*
Who'll buy, who'll buy, who'll buy, who'll buy?
A scientific instrument, a so-called gazing glass—
Stare at the ground and see the sky,
And cheaply anyone can see the dragon on his a—
At his feet!

(Everyone laughs quietly.)

FIRST CITIZEN: Ha ha, what a risky thing to say in the street!

SECOND CITIZEN: Don't hold your breath to see the dragon at your feet!

(They buy gazing glasses. Everyone looks into one, now that the crowd has broken up into groups.)

(The din of battle keeps growing fiercer.)

FIRST FEMALE CITIZEN: The situation's dire!

SECOND FEMALE CITIZEN: Poor Dragon's going for broke!

FIRST FEMALE CITIZEN: He isn't breathing fire!

SECOND FEMALE CITIZEN: He's only puffing smoke!

FIRST CITIZEN: The battle plan seems intricate—east, west, then north and south.

SECOND CITIZEN: If you ask me...no, never mind, I shouldn't open my mouth.

FIRST CITIZEN: I can't understand it.

HENRY: Stand by for a bulletin from the Independent Town Council. We are finalizing the battle. The enemy has lost his sword. His lance is out of commission. A moth has been detected in the flying carpet and faster than the eye can see it is boring through the enemy's air power. Cut off from his home base, the enemy cannot procure moth-balls and squashing the moth between his hands would force him to let go of the controls. Sir Dragon has made no move to exterminate the enemy solely out of a love of warfare. He has yet to fill his quota of anti-personnel manoeuvres or to exploit fully his own wonderful courage.

FIRST CITIZEN: Oh, now I understand.

LITTLE BOY: Momma, momma, look up in the sky,
The dragon's such a wreck!
All the time he's up so high
He gets it in the neck!

FIRST CITIZEN: Little boy, he's got three necks.

LITTLE BOY: Then he's getting it in all three necks.

FIRST CITIZEN: Optical illusion, little boy,
Your eyes are playing you tricks.

LITTLE BOY: These are tricks I can enjoy.
When I'm in fights, I count the kicks

And know who's beating who.
Ow! What's that?

FIRST CITIZEN: Take away the brat.

SECOND CITIZEN: What are we going to do?
I can't believe my very eyes!
Is there an oculist in the house?

FIRST CITIZEN: It's falling here from out the skies!
I can't stand the suspense!
Don't stand in my way, you louse!

(*The* DRAGON'*s head tumbles into the square with a crash.*)

MAYOR: A news bulletin! My kingdom for a news
bulletin!

HENRY: Stand by for a bulletin from the Independent
Town Council. His strength depleted, Lancelot has lost
and been partially taken prisoner.

LITTLE BOY: Why partially?

HENRY: Because. It's a military secret. His remaining
parts are resisting, but their ranks are broken. By
the way, Sir Dragon has released one of his heads
from active service on grounds of ill health. He has
appointed it to head the reserves.

LITTLE BOY: All the same I don't understand...

FIRST CITIZEN: What's not to understand? When you
were littler, did you ever
Lose a baby tooth?

LITTLE BOY: Sure.

FIRST CITIZEN: They all fall out, and even so
You're living. That's the truth.

LITTLE BOY: The loss of teeth I hardly feel,
But I never lost my head.

FIRST CITIZEN: Big deal.

HENRY: And now here's an analysis of the latest events. Flash: number-wise, why are two heads better than three? Two heads are allied to two necks. Two and two make four. It stands to reason. Besides which, they are inseparable allies.

(The DRAGON's *second head falls with a crash into the square.)*

HENRY: This analysis has been rescheduled on account of technical difficulties. Stand by for the latest bulletin. Military operations are escalating according to the game plan provided by Sir Dragon.

LITTLE BOY: Is that all?

HENRY: That's all for now.

FIRST CITIZEN: I've lost two-thirds of my respect for the Dragon. Master Charlemagne! Dear friend! Why are you standing over there all by yourself?

SECOND CITIZEN: Come over here by us.

FIRST CITIZEN: I can't believe the guards won't let you see your only daughter! How shocking!

SECOND CITIZEN: Why don't you speak up?

FIRST CITIZEN: Have we offended you in some way?

CHARLEMAGNE: No, but I'm confused. First you made no bones about not talking to me. That was clear enough. And now you make no bones about being pleased to see me.

GARDENER: Oh, Master Charlemagne. Don't trouble your head over that. Ain't it awful? Awful to think of the time I wasted, running to lick the paw of that one-headed monster. The flowers I could have grown!

HENRY: And now here's an analysis of the latest events!

GARDENER: Stop already! You're making us sick!

HENRY: Never you mind! This is wartime. You're
supposed to put up with everything. So here goes.
There is one God, one sun, one moon and one head on
the shoulders of our gallant victor. The possession of
a total of one head is a truly human trait, it's humane
in the best sense. Not to mention that, from a purely
military standpoint, it's shrewd tactics. It narrowly
limits the range of territory to be defended. One head
is twice as easy to defend as three.

(The DRAGON's *third head tumbles into the square with a
crash.)*

(A volley of shouts. Now everyone speaks very loudly.)

FIRST CITIZEN: Down with the Dragon!
His life was a crime!

SECOND CITIZEN: He cheated us from backside
Right up to breakfast-time.

FIRST FEMALE CITIZEN:
What a great feeling! No one to obey!

SECOND FEMALE CITIZEN:
I feel I've been drinking and drinking all day!

LITTLE BOY:
Momma, I bet school's been called off! Hooray!

PEDDLER:
Who'll buy, who'll buy, who'll buy, who'll buy?
A tiny dragon made of cardboard, treat it as you like.
Pluck off its wings, lop off its head,
Or step on the puny tyke.

HENRY: Stay tuned for the news bulletin!

EVERYONE: Our eyes are shut! And now we'll shout,
Whenever we feel like it! We'll bark,
Whenever we feel like it! What a lark!
I'm so drunk with joy I'm out of my wits,

And as for that boy *(Pointing to* HENRY*)* let's tear him to bits!

MAYOR: Hey! Guards!

(The guards rush into the square.)

MAYOR: *(To* HENRY*)* Go ahead. Start gently, and then pound it into 'em. Atten-hut!

HENRY: *(Very soothingly)* If you don't mind, please stand by the latest bulletin. Nothing, repeat, absolutely nothing of interest has occurred on any front. Everything is hunky-dory. A state of what you might call martial law has just been declared. If anyone is found spreading rumors *(Menacingly)*, off with his head, and no fines substituted! Got that? Everybody home! Guards, clear the square!

(The square empties out.)

HENRY: Well? How did you like that show?

MAYOR: Not so loud, sonny boy.

(A dull, heavy thud that makes the ground tremble.)

MAYOR: That's the dragon's body crashing to the ground behind the mill.

FIRST HEAD: Boy!

HENRY: Why are you rubbing your hands together, Pop?

MAYOR: Ah, sonny-boy! Power has just toppled into them.

SECOND HEAD: Mayor, come over to me! Give me some water! Mayor!

MAYOR: Everything's going swimmingly, Henry. The dear departed trained them to obey anybody who wields the whip-hand.

HENRY: But just now in the square...

MAYOR: Oh, that's nothing. Any dog will run around like crazy once it's let off the leash, and then it'll crawl back to its kennel on its own.

THIRD HEAD: Boy! Come here to me! I'm dying.

HENRY: But aren't you afraid of Lancelot, Pop?

MAYOR: No, sonny. You think it was easy to kill the dragon? Most likely Sir Lancelot is lying helpless on his flying carpet and the wind will carry him far from our town.

HENRY: But if he suddenly swoops down on us...

MAYOR: Then we'll settle his hash in no time. He's helpless, believe you me. Our dear departed knew how to fight, I'll say that for him. Let's go. We've got to draft our first proclamation. The main thing is to behave as if nothing whatever has happened.

FIRST HEAD: Boy! Mayor!

MAYOR: Let's go, let's go, there's no time to lose!

(HENRY and MAYOR leave.)

FIRST HEAD: Why, why did I smite him with my middle left paw? I should have used the middle right.

SECOND HEAD: Hey, anybody! You, Miller! You used to kiss my tail whenever we met. Hey, Friedrichsen! You once gave me a pipe with three mouth-pieces and the inscription "Forever thine". Where are you, Anna-Maria-Frederika Weber? You told me you were in love with me, and on your breast you wore clippings from my claws in a velvet sachet. We came to an understanding ages ago. Where are you all now? Give me some water. Look, the well is right beside me. Just a sip! Half a sip! At least wet my lips.

FIRST HEAD: Let me, just let me start over again! I'd smash every last one of you!

SECOND HEAD: One little droplet, somebody.

THIRD HEAD: I should have trained at least one loyal soul. But the material wasn't up to it.

SECOND HEAD: Hush! I sniff out a living being nearby. Come over here. Give me some water.

LANCELOT: *(Off)* I can't!

(And LANCELOT *appears in the square. He is standing on the flying carpet, leaning on a bent sword. In his hands is the cap of invisibility. At his feet is the musical instrument.)*

FIRST HEAD: You won by a fluke! If I had smote you with a middle right...

SECOND HEAD: Nevertheless, farewell!

THIRD HEAD: My one consolation is I'm leaving you charred souls, bed- wetting souls, dead souls... Nevertheless, farewell!

SECOND HEAD: Only one man around, the very man who killed me! What a way to go!

ALL THREE HEADS: *(In unison)* What a way to go. Farewell! *(They die.)*

LANCELOT: Now they're dead, but I don't feel at all well. My hands don't obey me. My sight is failing. And I keep hearing someone calling me by name: "Lancelot, Lancelot!" A familiar voice. A melancholy voice. I don't want to go. But I think I have to this time. What do you think, am I dying?

(The musical instrument replies.)

LANCELOT: Yes, to listen to you, it all had a sublime and noble ending. But I feel awfully sick. I'm mortally wounded. Wait a while, wait... But the Dragon is slain and that lets me breathe more easily. Elsa! I overcame him! True, I'll never see you again. Elsa! You won't smile at me or kiss me or ask me: "Lancelot, what's wrong? Why are you so sad? Why is your head spinning? Why do your shoulders ache? Who is calling

you so loudly—Lancelot, Lancelot?" It is Death calling
me, Elsa. I am dying. It's very depressing, isn't it?

(Musical instrument replies.)

LANCELOT: It's very upsetting. They've all gone into
hiding. As if a victory were some kind of disaster. Just
you wait, Death. You know me. I've looked you in
the face more than once and never went into hiding. I
won't run! I hear you. Give me one more little minute
to think things over. They've all gone into hiding.
All right. But now at home they're ever so gradually
coming to their sense. Their souls are straightening
out. Why, they're whispering, why did we feed and
tend that monster? Because of us a man is dying in the
town square, all, all alone. Well, now we'll be smarter!
What a battle that was, waged in the sky on our
account. How hard it is for poor Lancelot to breathe.
Oh no, enough is enough! On account of our frailty
the strongest, the most virtuous, the most audacious
men were dstroyed. Even stones would have got the
point. And we, after all, are human beings. That's what
they're whispering now in every house, in every little
room. Do you hear?

(Musical instrument replies.)

LANCELOT: Yes, yes, quite right. It means I'm not dying
in vain. Farewell, Elsa. I knew that I would love you
all my life long... But I didn't think my life would
end so soon. Farewell, town, farewell, morning, day,
evening. And now night is coming on! Hey, you! Death
is calling, rushing... My thoughts are in a tangle...
Something...something else I've got to say...Hey, you!
Don't be afraid. It can be done—you don't have to
injure widows and orphans. Pity for one another—that
can be done too. Don't be afraid! Pity one another.
Take pity—and you shall be happy! Word of honor, it's

the truth, the plain truth, the plainest truth there is on earth. And that's all. Now I'm going. Farewell.

(The musical instrument replies.)

(Curtain)

END OF ACT TWO

ACT THREE

(Luxuriously furnished hall in the MAYOR's *palace. Upstage, on either sides of the door, semi-circular tables laid for supper. Center, in front of them, a small table on which lies a hefty tome bound in gold. At the rise of the curtain, an orchestra strikes up. A group of* CITIZENS *is staring at the door and cheering.)*

CITIZENS: *(Quietly)* One, two, three. *(Loudly)* Long live the Dragon-slayer! *(Quietly)* One, two, three. *(Loudly)* Long live our hero! *(Quietly)* One, two, three. *(Loudly)* The joy we feel passes understanding! *(Quietly)* One, two, three. *(Loudly)* We hear his footsteps!

(Enter HENRY.*)*

CITIZENS: *(Loudly, but harmoniously)* Hip! Hip! Hurray!

FIRST CITIZEN: Oh, our Glorious Emancipator! Exactly one year ago you exterminated the accursed, antipathetic, insensitive and repulsive son of a bitch, the Dragon.

CITIZENS: Hip! hip! hurray!

FIRST CITIZEN: Even since then we have lived extremely well.

HENRY: Hold on, hold on, dear friends. Put the stress on "extremely."

FIRST CITIZEN: Righto. Ever since then we have livec exxx-tremely well.

HENRY: No, no, pal. Not like that. You mustn't emphasize the "ex". It might end up sounding like a hiss, very ambiguous. Just stress the "treme."

FIRST CITIZEN: Ever since then we have lived extreeeeemely well.

HENRY: By Saint George I think you've got it! That's the version I approve. After all, you know your Dragon-slayer. He's so modest a man he's practically naive. He loves sincerity and candor. Go on.

FIRST CITIZEN: We're simply out of our minds with joy.

HENRY: Excellent! Wait a minute. Let's put in something at this point that's...humanitarian, moral... The Dragon-slayer loves that sort of thing. *(Snaps his fingers.)* Hold on, hold on, hold on! It's coming, it's coming! It's coming! Aha! Got it! Even the dicky-birds are twittering merrily. Evil is fled and Good's at the head! Tweet-tweet! Tweet-hurray! Rehearse that.

FIRST CITIZEN: Even the dicky-birds are twittering merrily. Evil is fled—Good's at the head, tweet-tweet, tweet-hurray!

HENRY: That's a pretty limp tweet, pal! Be careful you don't get something to tweet about.

FIRST CITIZEN: *(Merrily)* Tweet-tweet! Tweet-hurray!

HENRY: That's a little better. Okay now. Have we already gone over the other bits?

CITIZENS: Yes, indeed, Mister Mayor.

HENRY: That's swell. Now the Dragon-slayer, President of our Free City, will be here any minute. Now remember—you've got to speak in unison but also frankly, humanely, democratically. The Dragon was big on ceremonials, but we...

SENTRY: *(From the center door)* At-tenshun! Door dress! His Excellency, Sir President of the Free City, is coming down the corridor. *(In a formulaic bass.)* Oh you sweetheart! Oh you knight in shining armor! You slew the Dragon! Can you imagine!

(Music strikes up. The MAYOR *enters.)*

HENRY: Your Excellency, Sir President of the Free City! During my stint of duty, nothing in particular has occurred! Ten men present. All of them insanely happy... Behind bars...

MAYOR: At ease, at ease, gentlemen. Good-day, Mayor. *(Shakes* HENRY's *hand)* Oh! And who are these? Eh, Mayor?

HENRY: Our fellow citizens are remembering that exactly one year ago you slew the dragon. They have come to offer congratulations.

MAYOR: Is that so? What a pleasant surprise! Well, lay it on me.

CITIZENS: *(Quietly)* One, two, three. *(Loudly)* Long live the Dragon-slayer! *(Quietly)* One, two, three. *(Loudly)* Long live our hero...

(The JAILER *enters.)*

MAYOR: Hold it, hold it! Good day, jailer.

JAILER: Good day, Your Excellency.

MAYOR: *(To the* CITIZENS*)* Thank you, gentlemen. I'm well aware of what you meant to say. Oh damn, an unbidden tear. *(Brushes away tear)* But then, you understand, there's to be a wedding in our house today, and I've still got a few little things to take care of. Be off with you, but come back later for the wedding. We'll have a real good time. The nightmare is past, and now we are living! Am I right?

CITIZENS: Hip! Hip! Hurray!

MAYOR: You got it. Slavery has entered the realm of legend, and we are reborn. Remember the sort of man

I was in that damned dragon's time? An invalid, a
lunatic. And now? Healthy as a horse. Not to mention
you. When I'm around, you're always merry and
bright, like dicky-birds. Well, fly away home. On the
double! Henry, show them out!

(*The* CITIZENS *depart.*)

MAYOR: Well, how's things in your jail?

JAILER: They're there.

MAYOR: And my ex-Deputy Mayor, how's he?

JAILER: Eating his heart out.

MAYOR: Ha! ha! No kidding?

JAILER: Honest to Pete, eating his heart out.

MAYOR: Yeah, but how?

JAILER: Crawling the walls.

MAYOR: Ha, ha! Serves him right! Nauseating type.
Used to be you'd tell a joke, everybody'd laugh, but
he'd say it was old and corny. Now let him sit and rot.
Did you show him my portrait?

JAILER: Sure did!

MAYOR: Which one? The one with my radiant smile?

JAILER: The very one.

MAYOR: And what'd he do?

JAILER: Cried.

MAYOR: No kidding?

JAILER: Honest to Pete, he cried.

MAYOR: Ha, ha! That's nice. And what about
those weavers who wove the magic carpet for...
whatshisname?

JAILER: I'm fed up with those bastards. They're on different floors, but they act as one. What one says so does the other.

MAYOR: But at least they've lost weight?

JAILER: In my shop people lose weight!

MAYOR: How about the blacksmith?

JAILER: He sawed through the bars again. I had to put a diamond window in his cell.

MAYOR: Fine, fine, don't spare the expense. So how's he now?

JAILER: Puzzled.

MAYOR: Ha, ha! That's nice!

JAILER: The hatter sewed little hats for the mice and now the cats won't go near 'em.

MAYOR: Oh yeah? Why not?

JAILER: They admire them. And the musician sings, it'd break your heart. Whenever I visit him, I stuff wax in my ears.

MAYOR: That's right. What about the town?

JAILER: Quiet. Although people're writing.

MAYOR: Writing what?

JAILER: The letter "L" on the walls. It stands for Lancelot.

MAYOR: Poppycock. L means Love Your President.

JAILER: Aha... In other words, don't imprison the writers?

MAYOR: Where'd you get that idea? Imprison them. What else do they write?

JAILER: It's embarrassing to say. The President is a Swine. His Son Is a Swindler... The President *(Giggles in a bass voice)* ...I don't dare repeat their graffiti. But most of all they write L.

MAYOR: A bunch of crackpots. They're obsessed with this Lancelot. No news of him, is there?

JAILER: Vanished.

MAYOR: Did you interrogate the birds?

JAILER: Uh-huh.

MAYOR: All of them?

JAILER: Uh-huh. Look at the mark the eagle gave me. Pecked off my ear.

MAYOR: Well, what do they say?

JAILER: They say they haven't seen Lancelot. One parrot did cooperate, I says to him: Seen him? And he says to me: Seen him. I says to him: Lancelot? And he says: Lancelot. But you know what parrots are like.

MAYOR: How about the snakes?

JAILER: If they knew anything, they'd have slithered in by now. They're on our side. Then too, they're relatives of the dear departed. But they haven't come crawling.

MAYOR: How about the fish?

JAILER: Not a word.

MAYOR: Maybe they know something?

JAILER: No. Expert fish specialists have looked them in the eye and come to a conclusion: they say they don't know a thing. In short, Lancelot, alias Saint George, alias Perseus the Barefoot—he's got a different monicker for every country—has hitherto not been located.

MAYOR: Then the hell with him.

(Enter HENRY.*)*

HENRY: The father of the happy bride, Keeper of the Public Records Charlemagne, is here.

MAYOR: Aha! Aha! I have to talk to him. Show him in.

(CHARLEMAGNE *enters.*)

MAYOR: All right, jailer, you may go. Keep up the good work. I'm pleased with you.

JAILER: We aim to please.

MAYOR: Keep aiming. Charlemagne do you know the Jailer?

CHARLEMAGNE: Not very well, Sir President.

MAYOR: 'Zat so. Never mind. Maybe you'll get to know him better soon.

JAILER: Arrest him?

MAYOR: Take it easy, there's plenty of time to arrest him. Go on, go away for now. See you soon.

(JAILER *exits.*)

MAYOR: Well now, Charlemagne, you've guessed, I'm sure, why we summoned you? All this political red tape has kept me from paying you a personal visit. But you and Elsa know from the proclamations posted throughout the city that today is her wedding day.

CHARLEMAGNE: Yes, we know it, Sir President.

MAYOR: We politicians haven't got the time to make proposals with flowers, deep sighs and the rest of that stuff. We don't propose, we dispose whatever has to be done. Ha, ha! Much more efficient that way. Elsa happy?

CHARLEMAGNE: No.

MAYOR: Oh, now what... Of course, she's happy. What about you?

CHARLEMAGNE: I am in despair, Sir President...

MAYOR: How ungrateful! I slew the Dragon...

CHARLEMAGNE: Forgive me, Sir President, but I cannot believe that.

MAYOR: Yes, you can!

CHARLEMAGNE: Word of honor, I can't.

MAYOR: You can, you can. If I can believe it, you certainly should be able to.

CHARLEMAGNE: No.

HENRY: He simply doesn't want to.

MAYOR: Why not?

HENRY: Waiting for the price to go up.

MAYOR: All right. I offer you the post of my Chief of Staff.

CHARLEMAGNE: I don't want it.

MAYOR: Don't be silly. You do want it.

CHARLEMAGNE: No.

MAYOR: Stop haggling, there's no time for that. A government apartment overlooking the park, nearby the market, a hundred and fifty-three rooms, and all windows with a southern exposure, by the way. Fabulous salary. And what's more, every time you go to the office, you get reimbursed for travel, and when you go home you get holiday pay. If you visit somebody, you get travel expenses, and if you stay home, you get a per diem. You'll be almost as rich as me. That's it. If you agree.

CHARLEMAGNE: No.

MAYOR: Then what do you want?

CHARLEMAGNE: All we want is not to be bothered, Sir President.

MAYOR: Oh that's dandy, that is—don't bother us! Suppose I want to? And anyway, what I'm doing is very profitable from a political point of view. The Dragon-slayer weds the girl he's saved. It's so convincing. Why won't you get it through your head?

CHARLEMAGNE: Why do you torment us? I had just learned how to think for myself, Sir President, which is agonizing enough, and then this wedding comes along. It's enough to drive a man mad.

MAYOR: Stuff and nonsense! All these psychiatric disorders are just so much piffle. Make-believe.

CHARLEMAGNE: Oh my God! How helpless we are! The town is every bit as meek and submissive as it ever was—it's ghastly.

MAYOR: What are you raving about? Why is it ghastly? What are you aiming at—you and your daughter plotting a revolt?

CHARLEMAGNE: No. She and I took a walk in the woods today and we were both so happy and talked it out in such detail. Tomorrow, as soon as she is no more, I shall die too.

MAYOR: What do you mean, when she is no more? What's this crap?

CHARLEMAGNE: You don't suppose that she will survive this wedding, do you?

MAYOR: Of course I do. It'll be a wonderful, delightful celebration. Anybody else would be overjoyed to marry his daughter to a rich man.

HENRY: And he is overjoyed.

CHARLEMAGNE: No I'm not. I'm up in years and I was taught to be polite. It's hard for me to say this straight out. But I have to say it, no matter what. This wedding is a calamity for us.

HENRY: What a tiresome way to drive a bargain.

MAYOR: Listen here, my friend! You aren't getting any more than what I've already offered. Obviously you want a piece of our action? Well, not a chance! Everything that the Dragon snatched so boldly is now in the hands of the city's foremost citizens. To wit, mine and, to some degree, Henry's. It's completely legal. And we aren't parting with a penny of it!

CHARLEMAGNE: May I be allowed to withdraw, Sir President?

MAYOR: Yes you may. Just keep this in mind. First, at the wedding, you will please to be merry, fun-loving and full of jokes. Second: nobody dies! Try hard to live as long as I see fit. Convey that to your daughter. Third: in future address me as "Your Excellency". You see this list? There are fifty names on it. All your best friends. If you go and mutiny, all fifty hostages will disappear without a trace. Go away. Hold on. I'll be sending a coach for you soon. You bring your daughter here—and no monkey business! Got me? Get out!

(CHARLEMAGNE *exits.*)

MAYOR: From here on in, it's smooth sailing.

HENRY: What did the jailer have to report?

MAYOR: Not a cloud on the horizon.

HENRY: What about the "L" on the walls?

MAYOR: Oh, you remember how much graffiti there was when the Dragon was in charge? Let 'em scrawl. It makes them feel better and it's no skin off our nose. Check and see if there's anybody in that chair.

HENRY: For crying out loud, pop! *(Feels the chair)* There's nobody in it. You can sit down.

MAYOR: It's no laughing matter. With that cap of invisibility he's got, he can sneak in anywhere.

HENRY: Pop, you don't know the man. He's up to his eyebrows in scruples. According to his code of chivalry, he'd have to take his cap off before he came inside,—and then the guards would catch him.

MAYOR: In a year's time he may have forgot his manners. *(Sits)* Now, sonny boy, you chip off the old block, let's get down to our private business. Like that little debt you owe me, sunshine!

HENRY: Which one's that, dad?

MAYOR: You bribed three of my flunkeys to dog my footsteps, read my personal mail, et cetera., et cetera. Am I right?

HENRY: The things you say, daddy!

MAYOR: Hold on, sonny, don't interrupt. I upped the ante five hundred thalers out of my own pocket so all they'd pass on to you was declassified information. Therefore you owe me five hundred thalers, you rascal you.

HENRY: No way, pop. Once I found out what you were doing, I upped it another six hundred.

MAYOR: And, figuring you'd try something like that, I went another thousand, you clever little swine! So the balance is in my favor. And don't raise the stakes any higher, kiddo. They're eating themselves blue in the face, getting out of shape and out of hand. If we don't watch out, they'll be turning on us soon. Another thing. You've really got to stop demoralizing my private secretary. I've had to send the poor guy to a psychiatric clinic.

HENRY: Is that so? What for?

MAYOR: Why, you and I were bribing him and counter-bribing him so many times a day, he couldn't keep straight who he was working for. He was sending me confidential reports on myself. He's been bugging his own conversations. He's a decent guy, and a hard worker, and it's a crying shame to see the stress he's under. Let's drop in on him tomorrow at the clinic and settle once and for all who his boss is. Ah, that's my boy! That's my great white hope! Wanted to wangle Daddy's job for his own self.

HENRY: How can you say that, pop?

MAYOR: 'S all right, junior! 'S all right. These things happen. You know what? Let's spy on one another plain and simple, keep it in the family, father and son, without all these middle-men. Think of the money we'll save!

HENRY: Oh, pop, money's got nothing to do with it!

MAYOR: True enough. You can't take it with you...

(The clatter of hooves and the jingle of bells)

MAYOR: *(Rushes to the window)* She's here! Our beauty's here! What a coach! A marvel! All adorned with dragon's scales. And Elsa in the flesh! Wonder of wonders. All in velvet. No, when you come down to it, power's a pretty good thing to have... *(Whispers)* Question her!

HENRY: Who?

MAYOR: Elsa. She's been so close-mouthed these last few days. Wonder if she knows where you-know-who is... *(Glancing round)* Lancelot. Question her carefully. And I'll be eavesdropping here behind this arras. *(Hides.)*

(Enter ELSA *and* CHARLEMAGNE.*)*

HENRY: Greetings and salutations, Elsa. You get prettier with every passing day—how nice of you to think of it. The President is changing and asks me to convey his apologies. Sit in this armchair, Elsa.

(HENRY *seats* ELSA *with her back to the arras behind which the* MAYOR *is hiding.*)

HENRY: And you can wait outside, Charlemagne.

(CHARLEMAGNE *bows and exits.*)

HENRY: Elsa, I'm glad the President is busy putting on his full regalia. For a long time now, I've wanted to be alone with you, just for a friendly chat, a heart-to-heart. Why don't you say something? Hmmmm? Won't you answer me? I'm very fond of you in my own way, you know. Talk to me.

ELSA: What about?

HENRY: Whatever you like.

ELSA: I don't know... There's nothing I want to say.

HENRY: There must be. After all, today's your wedding day... Ah, Elsa... Once again I'm forced to give you up to another. But to the victor belongs the spoils. I'm a wise-guy, a scoffer, but even I have to give him credit. Are you listening to me?

ELSA: No.

HENRY: Oh, Elsa... Have I really turned into such a stranger to you? Remember what good friends we were as children. Remember how you were down with the measles, and I'd come over and stand under your window so I could catch them too. And then you'd visit me and cry because I was so puny and under the weather. Remember?

ELSA: Yes.

HENRY: How can the children who were such good friends suddenly die? How can there be nothing left of them in us? Let's talk as we used to in days gone by, like brother and sister.

ELSA: All right, let's talk.

(The MAYOR *peeps out from behind the arras and noiselessly applauds* HENRY.)

ELSA: You want to know why I'm always silent?

(The MAYOR *nods his head.)*

ELSA: Because I'm afraid.

HENRY: Who of?

ELSA: People.

HENRY: Is that so? Let me know which people you're afraid of. We'll put 'em behind bars and you'll start to feel better right away.

(The MAYOR *takes out a notebook.)*

HENRY: Now, name names.

ELSA: No, Henry, that won't help.

HENRY: It will, I promise. This is the voice of experience. You'll sleep better, and your appetite will improve, and your frame of mind.

ELSA: Don't you see...I don't know how to explain it...I'm afraid of everyone.

HENRY: Aha, so that's it...I understand, I understand perfectly. You feel that everybody, me included, is hard-hearted. Right? You probably won't believe me but...I'm afraid of them myself. I'm afraid of my own father.

(The MAYOR *splays his hands in a gesture of bewilderment.)*

HENRY: I'm even afraid of our faithful servants. And I pretend to be so hard- hearted to make them afraid of me. Ah, we get all tangled up in webs of our own weaving. Go on, keep talking, I'm listening.

(The MAYOR *nods to show he understands.)*

ELSA: What more can I say... First I got angry, then I got depressed, and then I just stopped caring. And now

I'm as submissive as I ever was. Anyone can have his way with me.

(*The* MAYOR *giggles out loud. He hides in alarm behind the arras.* ELSA *looks around.*)

ELSA: Who was that?

HENRY: Pay no attention! They're setting up for the wedding banquet in there. My poor, dear little sister. What a shame that he vanished, that Lancelot vanished without a trace. I'm only now beginning to understand him. He was a wonderful person. We all did him an injustice. Is there no hope that he will return?

(*Once again the* MAYOR *creeps out from behind the arras. He's all ears.*)

ELSA: He...he will not return.

HENRY: You mustn't think that. Somehow I feel sure that we'll see him again.

ELSA: No.

HENRY: Believe me!

ELSA: I enjoy hearing you say it, but...can anyone overhear us?

(*The* MAYOR *squats down behind the back of her chair.*)

HENRY: Of course not, dearest. Today's a holiday. All the spies have the day off.

ELSA: Don't you see...I do know what became of Lancelot.

HENRY: Don't, not another word if it's painful for you.

(*The* MAYOR *shakes his fist at him.*)

ELSA: No, I've brooded over it in silence for so long that I feel like telling you everything now. I felt that I was the only one who realized how sad it all is—and yet I was born in this town. But you've been so kind and considerate today... Anyway... Exactly one year

ago, when the battle was over, the Cat ran to the Palace
square. And there he saw Lancelot, pale, pale as death,
standing by the Dragon's slain heads. He was leaning
on his sword and smiling, to keep from distressing
the Cat. The Cat hurried to me to bring help. But the
guards were keeping me so close that a fly couldn't
have flown in the house. They chased the Cat away.

HENRY: The brutes!

ELSA: Then he went for his friend the Donkey. After
laying the wounded man on the donkey's back, he led
them by the back alleys out of our town.

HENRY: But why?

ELSA: Oh, Lancelot was so weak that people might
have killed him. And so they took the trail to the
mountains. The Cat sat beside the wounded man and
listened for his heart-beat.

HENRY: It was still ticking, I should hope?

ELSA: Yes, but more and more faintly. And then the Cat
shouted, "Wait!" and the Donkey stopped. Night had
fallen by then. They had climbed high, high up into the
mountains and all around it was ever so quiet and ever
so cold. "Let's turn back!" said the Cat. "No one can
harm him now. Let Elsa pay her last respects and then
we'll bury him."

HENRY: He was dead, poor fellow!

ELSA: Dead, Henry. The obstinate Donkey said, "I don't
hold with turning back." And he trudged onward. But
the Cat did come back—cats are so fond of their homes.
He came back, told me all about it, and now I wait for
no one. It's all over.

MAYOR: Hurray! It's all over. (*He dances round the room.*)
It's all over! I'm high and mighty and the only show
in town! There's absolutely no one to fear any more.

Thanks, Elsa! This is a holiday! Now who's got the
nerve to say I didn't slay the dragon? Who, I ask you?

ELSA: He was eavesdropping?

HENRY: Of course.

ELSA: And you knew it?

HENRY: Oh, Elsa, skip the innocent maiden routine.
You're getting married today, thank God!

ELSA: Papa, Papa!

(CHARLEMAGNE *rushes in.*)

CHARLEMAGNE: What's wrong, my child? (*Tries to
embrace her*)

MAYOR: Hands off! Stand to attention in the presence
of my bride-to-be!

CHARLEMAGNE: (*At attention*) There, there, calm down.
Don't cry. What can anyone do? There's nothing
anyone can do. What can anyone do about it?

(*Music strikes up.*)

MAYOR: (*Runs to window*) Fantastic! A heart-warming
sight! Guests arriving for the wedding. The horses
caparisoned with ribbons! Japanese lanterns on the
carriages! Ain't it grand to be alive and know that
no fool can stand in your way. Flash us a smile, Elsa.
Any second now, when the proper time comes, the
President of this Free City himself will clasp you in his
embrace.

(*Doors swing wide open*)

MAYOR: Welcome, welcome, dear guests.

(*The* GUESTS *enter. They pass in couples past* ELSA *and the*
MAYOR. *They speak formally, almost in whispers.*)

FIRST CITIZEN: Congratulations to the bride and groom.
Everyone is overjoyed.

SECOND CITIZEN: The houses are decorated with
Japanese lanterns.

FIRST CITIZEN: The streets are as bright as day!

SECOND CITIZEN: The taverns are crammed with
people.

LITTLE BOY: Everyone's swearing and fighting.

GUESTS: Sssh!

GARDENER: May I present you with bluebells. It's true
they're ringing a bit mournfully, but never you mind.
By morning they'll be wilted and won't make a sound.

FIRST GIRL-FRIEND: Elsa, darling, try and cheer up.
Or else I'll start crying and smear my mascara, which
went on so smoothly today.

SECOND GIRL-FRIEND: After all, he's a lot better than
the Dragon... He's got arms and legs, and not a single
scale. After all, he may be the President, but he's still
human. You tell us all about it tomorrow. It'll be so
interesting.

THIRD GIRL-FRIEND: You'll be able to do so much good
for people! For instance, you could ask your husband
to fire my dad's boss. Then dad'll get his job and 'll
make twice as much money, and we'll be so happy.

MAYOR: *(Counting guests, sotto voce)* One, two, three,
four. *(Then place-settings)* One, two, three... Uh-oh...
One guest too many... Oh yes, it's the little boy... There,
there, stop whining. You can eat off your mommy's
plate. The gang's all here. Ladies and gentlemen, please
go to the table. We'll breeze through the marriage
ceremony without a lot of formalities, and then we'll
sit down to the wedding banquet. I've procured a fish
which was made to be eaten. It laughs with joy while
it's cooked, and informs the chef when it's done. And
here's a hen-turkey, stuffed with its own chicks. All
in the family, nice and cosy. And here are suckling

pigs, which were not only fed, but bred especially for
our table. They know how to sit up and offer a trotter,
even though they're roasted. Stop snivelling, little boy,
there's nothing scary about it, it's funny. And here's
some wine that's so old it's in its second childhood
and burbles like a baby in its bottles. And here's some
vodka that's been so distilled that the bottle looks
empty. Sorry, it really is empty. Those rascally flunkeys
cleaned it out. Well, never mind, there are lots more
bottles on the buffet. It's very nice to be rich, ladies and
gentlemen! Everybody seated? Splendid. Just a sec, just
a sec, only take a minute! Elsa! Gimme your paw!

(ELSA *extends her hand to the* MAYOR.)

MAYOR: You little rascal! You little kidder! What a
warm little paw! Let's see your kisser! Smile! All set,
Henry?

HENRY: You bet, Sir President!

MAYOR: Get on with it.

HENRY: Unaccustomed as I am to public speaking,
ladies and gentlemen, I'm afraid that what I'm about
to say may be a little messy. A year ago a puffed-
up vagabond challenged that damned Dragon to
mortal combat. A special commission, established
by the Independent Town Council, determined the
following: the deceased upstart had merely provoked
the deceased monster, by inflicting a harmless wound
on him. Thereupon, our ex-Mayor, now the President
of our Free City, heroically flung himself on the
Dragon and slew him, definitively this time, after
accomplishing sundry marvels of bravery.

(*Applause*)

HENRY: The thistle of ignoble slavery was torn up, root
and branch, from the top-soil of our social wheatfield.

(*Applause*)

HENRY: Our grateful city came to the following conclusion: if we used to bestow the finest maidens on that damned monster, the least we could do for our dear emancipator was to extend to him this simple and natural right!

(Applause)

HENRY: And therefore, to emphasize the greatness of our President, on the one hand, and the submissiveness and devotion of our city, on the other, I, in my capacity as Mayor, shall now perform the marriage ceremony. Organist, the wedding march!

(The organ sounds.)

HENRY: Scribes! Open the register of blessed events.

(Scribes with enormous fountain pens enter.)

HENRY: For four hundred years the names of the poor girls doomed to be the Dragon's have been inscribed in this book. Four hundred pages have been filled. And on page 401, for the very first time, we shall inscribe the name of a happy maiden, who is given in marriage to a doughty hero, the slayer of the monster.

(Applause)

HENRY: Bridegroom, make answer with clear conscience: wilt thou take this woman to be thy lawful wedded wife?

MAYOR: For the good of my native city I'm ready for anything.

(Applause)

HENRY: Scribes, put that down! Be very careful! If you make a blot, I'll have you lick it up! All right! That does it. Oops, sorry! There's still one trivial formality. Bride! Thou wilt, of course, take Sir President of this Free City as your lawful wedded husband? *(Pause)* Come on, spit it out, girl, wilt thou...

ELSA: No.

HENRY: Well, that's just fine. Scribes, write down, she will.

ELSA: Don't you dare write that!

(The SCRIBES *stagger backwards.)*

HENRY: Elsa, don't gum things up.

MAYOR: She's not gumming it up at all, my dear boy. If a girl says "no", she means "yes". Scribes, write it down!

ELSA: No! I'll tear the page out of the book and stamp on it!

MAYOR: Charming girlish indecision, tears, tantrums, that sort of thing. Every girl cries her eyes out before her wedding, and afterwards she's happy as the day is long. Now we'll take her by her little hand and do everything that has to be done. Scribes...

ELSA: At least let me make a statement! For pity's sake!

HENRY: Elsa!

MAYOR: No shouting, sonny. Everything's going according to plan. The bride requests the floor. Give her the floor and thereby conclude the formal proceedings. Never mind, never mind, let her—we're among friends.

ELSA: Friends, my friends! Why are you destroying me? It's horrible, a nightmare. When a bandit holds a knife to your throat, you might still escape. The bandit might be killed, or you might slip away from him... But what if the bandit's knife suddenly comes flying after you on its own? Or his rope slithers towards you, like a snake, to bind you hand and foot? What if even his window curtain, humble little window curtain, suddenly flung itself on you as well, to stifle your cries? What would you say then? I used to think that we all merely obeyed the Dragon the way the knife obeys the bandit. But you, my friends, turn out to be bandits too! I don't blame you, you are unaware of it yourselves, but I implore you—come to your sense! Suppose the Dragon didn't die but turned himself into a man, as he often did? Only this time he transformed himself into a mob of people, and now they are killing me. Don't kill me! Open your eyes! My God, the agony...Slice through the web in which you're all entwined. Isn't there anyone to stand up for me?

LITTLE BOY: I'd stand up for you, but Momma's got me by the hand.

MAYOR: Well, that's that. The bride has said her piece. Life goes on as before, no matter what.

LITTLE BOY: Momma!

MAYOR: Shush, little boy. Let's have a good time as if nothing had happened. Enough of this red tape, Henry. Write down, "The wedding is taken to be solemnized"—and let's eat. I could eat a horse.

HENRY: Scribes, write: the wedding is taken to be solemnized. Step on it! Why are you wool-gathering?

(The SCRIBES take up their pens. A loud knock at the door. The SCRIBES stagger backwards.)

MAYOR: Who's there? (Silence) Hey, you there! Tomorrow, whoever you are, come back tomorrow, during office hours, see my secretary. I'm busy now! I'm getting married!

(The doors fly open on their own. Nobody is at the door.)

MAYOR: Henry, come over here! What's the meaning of this?

HENRY: Oh, pop, it's the same old story. The innocent grievances of our maiden have stirred up all those simple-minded residents of the rivers, woods and

lakes. The house-goblin's left his attic, the water
sprite's crawled out of the well...Who cares?...What can
they do to us? They're just as invisible and powerless
as the so-called conscience and the rest of that stuff.
They'll bring us a couple of bad dreams and that'll be
the end of it.

MAYOR: No, he's here!

HENRY: Who is?

MAYOR: Lancelot. He's wearing his cap of invisibility.
He's standing right next to me. He's listening to what
we're saying. And his sword is dangling over my head.

HENRY: Daddy dearest! If you don't pull yourself
together, I shall seize power myself.

MAYOR: Music! Play! Dear guests! Please excuse this
unintentional hang-up, but I really worry about drafts.
A draft opened the door—and that's all there is to it.
Elsa, take it easy, sweety-pie. I proclaim the marriage
solemnized with that last formality. What's that?
Who's doing all that running?

(Panic-stricken FLUNKEY *runs in.)*

FLUNKEY: Take it back! Take it back!

MAYOR: Take what back?

FLUNKEY: Take back your damned money! I won't
work for you any more!

MAYOR: Why not?

FLUNKEY: He'll kill me for all the nasty things I've
done. *(Runs out)*

MAYOR: Who'll kill him? Huh? Henry?

*(*SECOND FLUNKEY *runs in.)*

SECOND FLUNKEY: He's already coming down the
corridor! I kowtowed to him and he didn't even

respond! He doesn't even look at people now. Oh, we're going to get it now! Oh, this it it! *(Runs out)*

MAYOR: Henry!

HENRY: Behave as if nothing were the matter. Whatever happens. That'll pull us through.

(THIRD FLUNKEY appears, backing in. Shouts into space)

THIRD FLUNKEY: I can prove it! My wife can testify to it! I always criticized their carrying-on! I only took their money on account of I'm neurotic. I'll get affidavits! *(Disappears)*

MAYOR: Look!

HENRY: Pretend nothing's happening! For God's sake, pretend nothing's happening!

(Enter LANCELOT.)

MAYOR: Oh, hello there, what a surprise. Still, even as an uninvited guest, welcome. We're short of china... but never mind. You can eat off this big plate, and I'll use the little one. I'd order them to set a fresh place, but those moron flunkeys have split... And here we were in the middle of getting married, so to speak, heh heh heh, just a little private party, so to speak. Nice and cosy.... Please, come and be introduced. Where in the world are the guests? Oh, they dropped something and are looking for it under the table. This is my son, Henry. I believe you've met. He's so young and already Mayor. He rose right to the top as soon as I... as soon as we... Well, that is, as soon as the dragon was slain. What's wrong? Please come in.

HENRY: Why don't you say something?

MAYOR: As a matter of fact, what is wrong? How was your journey? What's the good word? Wouldn't you like to lie down after your trip? The Guards'll show you the way.

LANCELOT: Hello, Elsa!

ELSA: Lancelot! *(Runs up to him)* Sit down, please sit down. Do come in. Is it really you?

LANCELOT: Yes, Elsa.

ELSA: And your hands are warm. And your hair's grown out since we last met. Or do I just think so? But the cloak is the same. Lancelot! *(Seats him at the small table center)* Have some wine. No, don't take anything from them. You shall rest and then we'll go. Papa! He's come, Papa! Just like that evening. Just when you and I were thinking that we were all alone in the world and the only thing left was to go and die without a sound. Lancelot!

LANCELOT: Does that mean you still love me as before?

ELSA: Papa, do you hear him? How many times did we dream that he would walk in and ask, "Elsa, do you still love me as before?" And I would reply, "Yes, Lancelot!" And then I would ask, "Where have you been so long?"

LANCELOT: Far, far away, in the Black Mountains.

ELSA: Were you terribly ill?

LANCELOT: Yes, Elsa. In fact, being mortally wounded is a very, very dangerous thing.

ELSA: Who cared for you?

LANCELOT: The wife of a woodcutter. A dear, kind woman. Though she was offended that in my delirium I kept calling her Elsa.

ELSA: Does that mean that you missed me?

LANCELOT: I did.

ELSA: And I was killing myself by degrees! They tormented me so.

MAYOR: Who did? Impossible! Why didn't you come
and complain to us? We would have done something
about it!

LANCELOT: I know all about it, Elsa.

ELSA: You do?

LANCELOT: Yes.

ELSA: How could you?

LANCELOT: In the Black Mountains, not far from the
woodcutter's cabin, there is an immense cave. And in
that cave there lies a book, the Book of Complaints,
filled with writing to the very end. No one puts a
finger on it, yet page after page is added to the earliest
writing, every single day. Who writes it? The world!
All the crimes of all the criminals, all the wretchedness
of those who suffer unjustly are written down.)

(HENRY *and the* MAYOR *tiptoe towards the door.*)

ELSA: And you read about us in there?

LANCELOT: Yes, Elsa. Hey, you there! Murderers! Stay
right where you are!

MAYOR: What cause have you to be so snappish?

LANCELOT: The cause is that I am not the man I was a
year ago. I liberated you and what did you do?

MAYOR: Oh, for heaven's sake! If you've got complaints
about me, I'll go into retirement.

LANCELOT: You're not going anywhere!

HENRY: Quite right. It's beyond belief the way he
carried on in your absence. I can supply you with a
complete list of his crimes, the ones that haven't got
in the Book of Complaints yet, because he was only
intending to commit them.

LANCELOT: Silence!

HENRY: Well, pardon me! If you investigate this thoroughly, you'll find I'm free of any personal responsibility. I was instructed to do it.

LANCELOT: Everyone was instructed. But why did you have to go to the head of the class, you swine?

HENRY: Let's go, dad. He's starting to use bad language.

LANCELOT: Oh no you don't. I've been back for a full month, Elsa.

ELSA: And you didn't come to see me!

LANCELOT: Yes I did, but in my cap of invisibility, early in the morning. I kissed you gently so that you wouldn't wake up. And I went for a stroll through the town. The life I saw was appalling. It had been hard enough to read about it but what I saw with my own eyes was harder still. Hey, you, Miller!

(FIRST CITIZEN *gets up from under the table.*)

LANCELOT: I saw you weeping with ecstasy when you shouted at the Mayor, "Long live the Dragon-slayer!"

FIRST CITIZEN: That's true. I did weep. But I wasn't pretending, Sir Lancelot.

LANCELOT: But didn't you know that he hadn't slain the dragon?

FIRST CITIZEN: In private I knew it...but in public... (*Splays his hands.*)

LANCELOT: Gardener!

(GARDENER *gets up from under the table.*)

LANCELOT: Did you teach your snapdragons to cry, "Hooray for the President!?"

GARDENER: I did.

LANCELOT: And did they learn it?

GARDENER: Yes. But whenever they did it, every snapdragon would stick its tongue out at me. I thought I'd try and get a government grant for fresh experiments...but...

LANCELOT: Friedrichsen!

(SECOND CITIZEN *crawls out from under the table.*)

LANCELOT: When the Mayor got angry with you, did he clap your only son in a dungeon?

SECOND CITIZEN: Yes. And the boy never stops coughing, dungeons being so damp!

LANCELOT: And yet, after that, you gave the Mayor a pipe with the inscription "Ever thine"?

SECOND CITIZEN: What else could I do to soften his heart?

LANCELOT: What am I to do with you?

MAYOR: Spit on them. It's not your job. This work is cut out for us. Henry and I will take care of them just beautifully. That'll be the best punishment for that riffraff. You take Elsa by the hand and leave us to go on as before. It'll be ever so humanitarian and democratic.

LANCELOT: I can't. Come in, friends!

(*Enter* WEAVERS, BLACKSMITH, HATTER *and* MUSICAL-INSTRUMENT MAKER.)

LANCELOT: Even you made me sore. I thought you'd know how to handle them when I wasn't around. Why did you truckle to them and end up in prison? There were plenty of you, weren't there?

WEAVERS: They didn't give us time to think.

LANCELOT: Take these people away. The Mayor and the President.

WEAVERS: (*Take hold of the* MAYOR *and* PRESIDENT) Get going!

BLACKSMITH: I tested the bars personally. Tough ones. Get going!

HATTER: Here are some dunce caps for you! I used to make such beautiful hats, but you and your prison have embittered me. Get going!

MUSICAL-INSTRUMENT MAKER: In my cell I carved a fiddle out of black bread and spun strings from a spider's web. My fiddle plays mournfully and softly, but that's your fault. Now you'll march to our tune to the place of no return.

HENRY: But this is ridiculous, it's irregular, people don't do such things. A bum, a derelict, a man with no practical training—and suddenly...

WEAVERS: Get going!

MAYOR: I protest, it's inhumane!

WEAVERS: Get going!

(Gloomy, simple, barely audible music. HENRY *and the* MAYOR *are led off.)*

LANCELOT: Elsa, I'm not the man I used to be. Can you see that?

ELSA: Yes. But I love you more than ever.

LANCELOT: We won't be able to go away...

ELSA: Never mind. We can enjoy ourselves at home.

LANCELOT: There's some minor business to clear up. More intricate than making lace. The Dragon has to be killed in each and every one of them.

LITTLE BOY: Will you hurt us?

LANCELOT: Not you.

FIRST CITIZEN: What about the rest of us?

LANCELOT: I'm going to have to take you in hand.

GARDENER: But be patient, Sir Lancelot. I entreat you—be patient. Make grafts. Kindle a bonfire—warmth promotes growth. Uproot the weeds carefully to make sure you don't injure the healthy roots. You know, when you think about it, people really and truly, maybe, when all's said and done, require very careful tending.

FIRST GIRL-FRIEND: And let's have a wedding today anyhow.

SECOND GIRL-FRIEND: Because people also improve when they're happy.

LANCELOT: That's true! Strike up the music!

(The music strikes up.)

LANCELOT: Elsa, give me your hand. I love all of you, my friends. Otherwise, what would be the point of bothering with you. And if I love you, everything will go splendidly. And after our long trials and tribulations we shall all be happy, very happy at the last!

(Curtain)

END OF PLAY